Practitioner Research
for Teachers

Diana Burton was a humanities teacher and head of year in a large comprehensive school before moving to work in teacher education at Manchester Metropolitan University where she became Head of Education Programmes. Now Dean of the Faculty of Education, Community and Leisure at Liverpool John Moores University, her areas of research and publication include differentiation and cognitive style, identity issues within teacher education and the professional development of teachers. She has published in various education journals and books on teacher education. Diana is co-author of *Introduction to Education Studies* (Paul Chapman Publishing, 2001) and co-editor of *Education Studies: Essential Issues* (Sage, 2003).

Steve Bartlett was a social studies teacher and head of department in a large comprehensive school before becoming an area co-ordinator and advisory teacher for the Technical Vocational Educational Initiative. He has since worked as a senior lecturer at Wolverhampton University where he became subject leader for education studies. He is currently Reader in Education at University College Chester. His areas of research and publication include the professional development of teachers, action research and education studies. Steve is co-author of *Introduction to Education Studies* (Paul Chapman Publishing, 2001) and co-editor of *Education Studies: Essential Issues* (Sage, 2003). He has worked for many years alongside teachers conducting practitioner research and has published widely in this field.

Practitioner Research for Teachers

Diana Burton
and Steve Bartlett

P·C·P
Paul Chapman
Publishing

First published 2005

 Paul Chapman Publishing
A SAGE Publications Company
1 Oliver's Yard
55 City Road
London EC1Y 1SP

SAGE Publications Inc
2455 Teller Road
Thousand Oaks, California 91320

SAGE Publications India Pvt Ltd
B-42, Panchsheel Enclave
Post Box 4109
New Delhi 110 017

Library of Congress Control Number: 2004104958

A catalogue record for this book is available from the
British Library

ISBN 0 7619 4420 6
ISBN 0 7619 4421 4 (pbk)

Typeset by Dorwyn Ltd, Wells, Somerset
Printed in Great Britain by the Athenaeum Press, Gateshead

Contents

Figures

Acknowledgements

We wish to thank the following practitioner researchers for allowing their research to be used as examples: Jacky Bennison, Padgate High School; Ray Elliott and Amanda Brand, Elleray Park School; Claire Realff, Stockton Heath Primary School; Carole Owens, Bruche Community Infant School; Amanda Isaac-Meurig, Angela McGovern, Steve Tones, Linda Rush, Tony Pickford.

We would also like to thank Mrs Vera Burton; Liverpool John Moores University Library and School of Education; and Captain Webb Primary School for reference to their materials.

A major part of Chapter 4 has previously been published as Bartlett, S. and Burton, D. (2003) 'The professional development of teachers through practitioner research: a discussion using significant cases of best practice research scholarships', *Teacher Development*, 7(1): 107–20.

■ ■ ■ Chapter 1

Teacher professionalism, development and research

■ ■ ■ Why are we writing this book?

We are interested in practitioner research because we engage in it our-selves and we work with teachers and teacher educators who are steeped in it. We also come from a generation of teachers who started their careers when it was mostly teachers themselves who decided what they taught, how they taught it and why they taught it that way. It is easy to romanticize and, of course, there were examination syllabi to follow and agreed protocols to guide us. We enjoyed the freedom, though, to develop from scratch an integrated humanities scheme of work for lower school (Key Stage 3) pupils; to set and mark our own mode 3 Certificate of Secondary Education (CSE) examinations; to experiment with com-pletely integrated days for 11–14-year-olds and to grow sociology from a one teacher subject to a whole department teaching 350 pupils annually. We wrestled with the philosophical basis of the 'core' curriculum, argued about the purpose and value of mixed ability groupings and had debates on teaching style with Her Majesty's Inspectorate (HMI) inspectors. OK, enough reminiscing!

We found those exciting times but now, with the great advances in our understanding of how people learn, the availability of fantastic learning technologies, the ubiquity of more varied and stimulating teaching strategies, the development of cross-curricular teaching projects and the welcome return of an emphasis on creativity in the curriculum, we are seeing that excitement rekindled and magnified. In recent years interest in practitioner teacher research has accelerated across the world and, with the shrinking of distances via electronic communication, the globalization of teaching strategies and research methodologies is common-place. Communities of like-minded practitioners can share their experiences and extend their understanding in international as well as very local contexts. So we are writing this book because we are excited about the potential of practitioner research to make a vital contribution to the collective, collaborative endeavour of enquiring about and improving teaching and learning practices. We are writing it as teachers, with teachers and for teachers, whether they are in training, beginning their careers or established crafts people.

■ ■ ■ What does this book do?

In setting out to write this book on practitioner research we were faced with an initial dilemma. It is our contention that practitioner research and professional development are heavily interrelated so it is difficult to know where to start, since in considering one aspect first, some knowl-edge of the rest has to be assumed. We have imposed a form of order by considering the theoretical underpinnings of practitioner research in the early chapters, and dealing with the practical aspects of research in the remainder of the book. This is an organizational device and not a privi-leging of theory over practice.

In Chapter 2 we discuss current conceptions of educational research. The UK government would like to promote research that is directly applicable to practice that identifies the 'best' approach so that teachers, who are now encouraged to consider empirical evidence, can implement it. The promotion of practitioner research now takes this process a stage further by encouraging teachers themselves to become the researchers into their practice. This is certainly a positive development; however, the version of classroom that it promotes remains rather narrow. This is, of course, not the only interpretation of practitioner research. It can also be conceptualized as a process whereby teachers are looking critically not only at their own practice but at broader educational questions. In this version of practitioner research a greater understanding of the complex-ity of education, and a realization of how uncertain the whole education project is, assumes ascendancy. The paradigms that underpin the research process, along with a consideration of some fundamental research concepts, are also discussed in this chapter. A penchant for the positivist paradigm tends to characterize government-sponsored practitioner research. This is perhaps due to a rather instrumentalist view that assumes only one approach to research, overwhelmingly quantitative in nature, will lead to the discovery of the 'correct' results. However, in beginning their research projects the limitations of this single paradigm approach becomes apparent to many practitioners.

Chapter 3 considers the growth of the teacher research movement through action research. This is seen as an enlightened research-based approach to teaching. Action research tends not to be universally embraced in 'official' versions of practitioner research, perhaps because of its stress on a broad approach to teacher development. Ultimately, the development of the current practitioner research movement will depend upon how effectively teachers are able to articulate the research process and how much autonomy they have in steering their own professional interests. Three case studies of best practice researchers and their movement towards different research approaches from those originally envisaged are used to illustrate these points in Chapter 4.

The remaining chapters examine the practicalities of designing a research project, accessing and reviewing literature and gathering and analysing data. Our approach is to describe and explain these processes through practical, real-life examples of research undertaken by teacher practitioners. We are proposing that practitioner research should form part of a reflexive approach to teaching and lead to a greater awareness of the complexity of the education process.

We have been privileged to work with people who have generously allowed us to extract from and comment upon their studies to illustrate in a practical way how and why teacher research can be tackled. We hope the book demonstrates how small-scale research projects might be tackled and whets readers' appetites to consult more authoritative research texts if they wish to develop a deeper engagement with the principles, processes and problematics of research. The suggested readings and reference list provide a good starting point and attempting some of the tasks at the end of each chapter may help the juices to flow!

We turn now to two discussions that will set the context for the remainder of the book. In the 1980s and 1990s there have been fierce debates about the nature and value of educational research and about the changing nature of teacher professionalism.

■ ■ ■ A crisis in educational research

Academic research in education has been criticized for a number of reasons in recent years. In the Teacher Training Agency (TTA) Annual Lecture of 1996, David Hargreaves, an influential UK educationalist, highlighted what he saw as the failure of educational research to serve those working in education. He called for teaching to become a research-based profession similar to medicine. He suggested that teachers at that time made little use of research evidence to inform their practice, through no fault of their own but because researchers were not producing findings that supported practice. Hargreaves (1996) suggested that current educational research was poor value for money and that it inadequately served the teaching profession. He called for the setting up of a National Education Research Forum 'which would shape the agenda of educational research and its policy implications and applications' (1996: 6). He also suggested that funding should be redirected from academic researchers to agencies committed to evidence-based practice and to fund teachers as researcher practitioners. This speech, whilst promoting heated debate amongst both academics and professionals concerned with education, was a forerunner of the TTA policy that promoted practitioner research (TTA, 1996) and an initial pilot project encouraging teachers to conduct their own practice-based research. The work of one of three TTA-funded projects from this time is outlined in McNamara (2002). The book shows how the researchers had to engage in a process of discussion and negotiation with their funders to reach a mutually agreeable position on a number of issues of ideological difference. McNamara and Rogers (2002) explained that the TTA moved from being sponsors to partners in the research process.

Both the Tooley Report (Tooley and Darby, 1998) funded by the Office for Standards in Education (OFSTED), and the Hillage Report (Hillage et al., 1998) funded by the Department for Education and Employment (DfEE), also raised questions concerning the quality and usefulness of educational research. Hammersley (2002) and Elliott (2001) argue that these criticisms, Hargreaves's in particular, all take a rather simplistic view of how research is able to inform practice. They assume that causal relationships can be revealed by research and that findings can be easily applied to all schools. This would mean that variables can be identified and allowed for, ignoring the complexity of what actually happens in classroom situations. Both Hammersley and Elliott maintain that what is essentially a positivist approach suitable for medical research is inappropriate in educational investigations. They also suggest that there is a values dimension to education that a natural scientific methodology looking for absolute answers fails to recognize. Elliott suggests that acquiring the questioning approach of a researcher is an essential part of teacher development. We should treat the whole research process as problematic with teachers taking a more interpretivist approach to classroom research rather than the positivist one which was inferred from Hargreaves's speech.

If, as Hammersley (2002) and others argue, there are different forms of research that are carried out for different purposes, it could be claimed that their outcomes should be evaluated differently because they offer complementary strengths and weaknesses. However, there is a danger that this could exacerbate the 'hierarchy' of research outputs that already exists. Greenbank (2003) points to how policy-makers, such as the former Secretary of State for Education, David Blunkett, hold quantitative research in higher esteem simply because of the way it is presented and to the assumption by the former Chief Inspector, Chris Woodhead, of qualitative research as 'woolly and simplistic' and a 'massive waste of taxpayers' money' (cited by Wellington, 2000: 167). There also exists a hierarchy in terms of where educational research is disseminated. 'Academic' peer-reviewed education journals of national or international repute do not publish professionally oriented research – this finds expression through professional publications, conferences and in-service courses. Since Hargreaves (1996) questioned the relevance of 'academic' educational research to teachers, the complexity of the debate has been revealed, imbued as it is with political tensions around research funding policies and the hijacking of so-called professional, accessible research in pursuit of the ill-defined populist agenda of raising standards. In an article describing the work of a community of teacher researchers in Denbigh, Evans et al. (2000) are scathing about the difficulties of getting teacher research published in academic journals and books that purport to talk with authority on schools, education and teaching and learning processes. Notwithstanding the differences in emphases of different types of research, there is every reason and every need, in our view, to assign parity of status to 'professional' and 'academic' research since practitioner research must be every bit as rigorous and is almost certainly at least as relevant.

■ ■ ■ Teachers as professionals

In embarking on any project it is important to set a context and try to develop some shared meanings. Thus, because we take the view that teacher practitioner research is inextricably linked with professional development, we will spend the remainder of this chapter considering the nature of teachers' work and the political context in which the term 'professional' is applied to them. Recent political developments within education are germane here since these have directly influenced current notions of teacher professionalism, teacher development and teacher research.

There is currently great emphasis on the continuing professional development of teachers. However it is important to distinguish between a narrow, technicist, or 'technical rational' (Habermas, 1974) view of teacher development and a broad approach that is more likely to lead to significant educational improvements. The raising of educational standards has been linked, in part, to the performance of teachers and has resulted in the UK in changes to the structure and funding for professional development. The government approach, as in many other parts of the world, tends to be largely instrumentalist, viewing education as a product to be used in social and economic development and teaching as imparting the proscribed curriculum to pupils. The most effective teaching methods can be identified and then applied. From this perspective teaching is very much a technical activity and so the means of researching it tend also to be conceived of as technical or mechanistic.

The role of the teacher is, however, very complex, embracing a multitude of skills (Squires, 1999; Sugrue and Day, 2002). What constitutes 'good' teaching is still very much open to debate and depends very much on particular circumstances (see Bartlett et al., 2001, for a discussion of this). Some people may argue that teaching involves a transfer of knowledge to pupils. Others may emphasize the teacher's role in facilitating learning. What is learned and how it is learned depends upon a range of factors, from the teacher's pedagogic beliefs to the syllabus being followed. For instance, infrequently facts are required to be reproduced verbatim so they may be learned by rote. For other knowledge pupils may conduct experiments or apply ideas to new problems. Developing certain skills will probably be done through practice and repetition. Thus 'lessons' can take many forms depending upon the professional judgements of the teacher (Burton, 2001; Hayes, 2000). However, education involves much more than the development of knowledge and skills. It has a very important moral and social dimension, in which teachers care for the pupils' welfare and foster the values of mutual respect and tolerance required in a democratic society.

The term 'profession' is frequently applied to the work of teachers but what does this actually mean and to what extent can teachers be regarded as professionals? Becker (1962) saw professionalism as merely a symbol for an ideology used to justify actions and behaviours, with many occupations using the symbol in an attempt to increase their autonomy and prestige. Many researchers have attempted to identify the features of a profession. Bottery (1996) suggested that at least 17 different criteria have been claimed at one time or another to describe professional behaviour. Salient characteristics included subscription to an exclusive, specialized body of knowledge partly learned in higher education, a code of professional conduct and ethics with a strong emphasis on service and a high degree of self-regulation by the professional body itself over entry, qualifications, training and members' conduct.

Looking at the past 50 years we could probably say that the teaching force embodied a number of these characteristics until the end of the 1970s. Teaching was seen as a worthwhile occupation and teachers were generally well respected within communities. As workers, teachers had enviable autonomy and independence but this was to alter radically through the 1980s and 1990s. Concern with 'standards' of learning led to 'The Great Debate' inspired by Callaghan's Ruskin speech in 1976. On gaining power in 1979 the Conservatives embarked on a radical programme of educational change predicated on free-market principles of greater parental choice and institutional autonomy. Coupled with this, paradoxically, was greater emphasis on public accountability and centralized curricular control. Policy changes such as the introduction of increasingly prescriptive curricula, publicly available school inspection reports, the publishing of pupil performance in league tables and the encouragement of bureaucratic management systems served to regulate the autonomy of teachers. Throughout the Conservative administrations of the 1980s and 1990s teachers' ability to control the pace, content, volume and assessment of their work declined (Ozga and Lawn, 1988). Routine administrative tasks grew in number. Schools' managements became more supervisory and concerned with performance levels, in keeping with their industrial counterparts. Teaching posts became less secure with redundancy, redeployment and retraining issues attacking the professional identity of teachers.

Describing professionals such as teachers prior to these policy changes Schön (1983) said the modern professional constantly questioned and reflected upon practice. This approach involved evaluation, criticism and, ultimately, self-development and required openness and trust between collaborating practitioners. Teachers were free to develop and trial critical and innovative approaches in their teaching. However, these high levels of autonomy did not sit easily with the managerialist forms of control that derived from Conservative free-market policies in the 1980s. School managers began to prize uniformity and predictability in their quest for the higher standards demanded by the government.

In analysing teacher professionalism, Hoyle (1980) differentiated broadly between 'restricted' and 'extended' professionals. The former could be described as conscientious practitioners who work hard, prepare their lessons and care about their pupils. However, they are limited in outlook, failing to think beyond their classroom or school. They do not consider the broader purposes of education as relevant to them. Extended professionals constantly question and try to link theory to practice, seeking to improve by learning from other teachers and engaging in professional development activities. In this way they are continually developing as teachers and placing their classroom work in a wider educational context. Hoyle argued that extended professionals show, in their search for fulfilment, greater potential. He advocated that this model of professionalism should be the aim of all teachers.

However, in a context where education was increasingly being seen as a commodity in the marketplace, forms of industrial management came to be considered applicable to schools. Management cultures emphasizing cost-effectiveness, efficiency and competition competed with professional cultures, which prioritize the development of the individual pupil, social relationships and collegiality. As managerialism became more salient, the notion of 'senior management' as distinguished from 'middle management' arose (Grace, 1995) and teachers became differentiated into a clearer hierarchy. Ozga (1995) suggested that the growth of management teams and supervisory functions may have 'extended' the professionalism of some but deskilled others. By this time teachers were uniformly experiencing increasing workload, progressive loss of control over their work and greater accountability to managerial forms of control.

Within education Hoyle (1995) observed that the meaning and use of the term 'professionalism' had altered. The focus was now in, and not beyond, the classroom. It had come to mean a form of management-assured quality delivery. Dale (1989) noted that teachers had moved from licensed autonomy, trusted by the state and allowed relative independence, to a more regulated autonomy, subject to greater external monitoring. Ozga (1995; 2000) characterized teachers as bureaucratized, state professionals. The state had effectively retained strategic control of teaching, the curriculum and assessment while, under the guise of empowerment and collegiality, teachers were subject to increasing monitoring and surveillance.

■ ■ ■ The 'new professionalism'

Labour's tenure has heralded little real policy change in education since the party came to power in 1997 with modernizing education as a central plank of their political agenda. An emphasis on partnership to raise standards, some increased funding for education and a new strategy for teacher professional development have been Labour's bargaining chips for securing teachers' flexibility and co-operation in the modernizing of the profession and raising of standards (see DfEE, 1997; 1998; DfES, 2001). However, apart from different spending priorities, most of the Conservative reforms have been left in place (Docking, 2000). Given the shortage of teachers, especially in key subject areas, and the importance of the teaching force in delivering Labour's reforms, there have been attempts to improve the public image and status of these 'new professionals' through, for example, such initiatives as the establishment of the General Teaching Council for England (GTCE), the creation of a National College for School Leadership (NCSL) and the awarding of knighthoods for chosen headteachers (McCulloch, 2001). In Scotland the McCrone Report was set up in 1999 to address similar concerns, with an emphasis on continuing professional development (CPD) as a means of ensuring a committed, flexible teaching force.

A major review of teacher professional development in England and Wales was launched in 2000, which sought to 'transform educational standards and raise achievement in every school' (DfEE, 2000a: 3). It was predicated on 10 principles: these included a need for teachers to take

ownership of their development, to 'learn on the job' from expert practitioners, to harness the potential of information and communication
technology (ICT) and to plan and evaluate their development programmes. The government pledged a commitment to fund and support
teachers' professional development through a culture of entitlement.
The training of senior and middle managers for schools through NCSL
bespoke programmes is now threatening to replace the traditional
master's degree qualification that aspiring school leaders formerly undertook. Thus training and teacher development now takes place
increasingly within a tightly managed school environment rather than
as part of higher education. The professional development of serving
teachers has become far more practical and focused and there is less
opportunity for teachers to extend their broader thinking as educationalists. The current emphasis for teacher development is on training as
opposed to education, and inspections of the quality of this training
scrutinize closely its impact on pupil progress (OFSTED, 2002). Fundamentally the goal is to raise standards of pupil achievement and the
emphasis is on the techniques of teaching. Patrick et al. (2003) explain
that a similar approach had been taken in Scotland; they contend that
the type and quality of CPD provided to teachers depends on whether
policy-makers are seeking to extend professional autonomy and practice
or to enhance performativity. In both countries at present the focus
appears to be on the latter goal.

A focus on teaching techniques has been encouraged by the vogue for
developing 'evidence-based practice' (see TTA, 1996). This can be interpreted as doing what has been shown to work and ignoring different
ideological approaches to teaching. Whilst desirable in aiming to
improve the craft of teaching, this approach is narrowly focused (Bottery
and Wright, 1999). There is little scope for reflection beyond the classroom and for wider pedagogical debate and it remains a
technical–rational approach to teaching, consistent in ideology with the
heavily prescriptive performance management system introduced progressively since 2000 to plan and deliver targets at school, subject and
pupil levels (see Bartlett and Burton, 2003). A key feature of this system
is the monitoring of pupil results, which is controversial in its assumption of a simplistic causal relationship between teacher input and pupil
attainment. In Hoyle's terms (1995) it encourages restricted rather than
extended professionalism. Changing conceptions of the nature of

teacher professionalism can be found extensively across the world; in each case the driver for change seems to be a political will for more superficially measurable outcomes (see Patrick et al., 2003, for more detail).

Essentially then, we have a context where the terms 'teacher professionalism' and 'teacher professional development' are used liberally but understood differently by the various stakeholder groups, including government agencies, policy-makers, teachers, teacher educators, school leaders and researchers. Whitty (1999: 2) suggests that it is best to see such alternative conceptions or models of teacher professionalism existing as competing versions rather than 'seeing any one as fitting an essentialist definition ... and others as detracting from it'. Individuals will support different versions as they are influenced by their political beliefs, values and position in relation to government reforms. Stronach et al. (2002) criticize the reductive typologies and characterizations of professionalism that can be seen, for example, in the HayMcBer report (available at www.dfee.gov.uk/teachingreforms/mcber), and argue for an account of professional identities that recognizes 'the local, situated and indeterminable nature of professional practice, and the inescapable dimensions of trust, diversity and creativity' (2002: 119). This captures very well the complexity of teachers' work and the fundamental nature of teachers developing professionally within their working environments in collaboration with colleagues. Practitioner enquiry is an extremely effective means of pursuing and supporting this professional development.

■ ■ ■ Task: Analysing the purpose of practitioner research

Read *Schools Achieving Success* (DFES, 2001).
Analyse:

1. How the work of teachers as professionals is portrayed here and what it involves.
2. The purpose of practitioner research as outlined in this document?

■ ■ ■ Suggested further reading

Craft, A. (2000) *Continuing Professional Development: A Practical Guide for Teachers and Schools*. 2nd edn. London: RoutledgeFalmer.

The author considers principles and models of the professional development of teachers. She investigates the planning and evaluation of both school and individual teacher development and as such this book will prove relevant and very interesting to the practitioner researcher.

Whitty, G. (2002) *Making Sense of Education Policy*. London: Paul Chapman Publishing.

This book considers education policy throughout the 1990s. It outlines curriculum innovation, teacher professionalism and school improvement. Whitty evaluates Labour education policy in terms of its fostering of social justice and inclusion. Though challenging, this is an interesting book for those working in education who are seeking a political overview.

■ ■ ■ Chapter 2

Defining educational research

■ ■ ■ Introduction

This chapter discusses the meaning of the term 'research' and shows how it forms part of our daily lives. The characteristics of formal research are outlined and different typologies of educational research identified. We then move to a discussion of the major paradigms that underpin research design and consider a number of key constructs that inform our research approaches.

■ ■ ■ What is research?

The term 'research' may seem initially daunting to 'beginners' until they realize that they are already used to gathering data in many ways on a daily basis as a normal part of their lives. The methods typically used to find things out include observing situations or particular events, listening to the radio, asking different people, looking things up in books or surfing the World Wide Web. All of this normal activity is data collection. We do it to make sense of the world in which we exist. Thus teachers and pupils are constantly 'interpreting' what is going on around them in the classroom. They carefully listen, observe and wait for responses to specific actions.

The data-gathering process may become slightly more formal and clearly defined, for instance when a teacher needs to write a pupil report for parents. This may involve the gathering of data from several sources. They are likely to look at recent work by the pupil, consider test results and consult with other members of staff. Another data-gathering task is when teachers carefully question several pupils to find out what happened in a particular incident. The experienced teacher realizes the subtle differences that would result in the information gathered when pupils are questioned individually, in pairs or in groups. Teachers are also aware of how to ask the questions differently depending upon the particular circumstances and their knowledge of the pupils involved. Clearly then, different methods of gathering information are appropriate to different situations. As new information becomes available to teachers in their daily lives concerning their teaching, pupils and other colleagues, they are constantly checking, modifying, refining and developing what they know. Some information received carries more weight with us than alternative sources of evidence. When questioning pupils about a particular incident the information gathered may vary and even conflict so teachers may expect to hear rather different accounts. Using different accounts often helps to provide teachers with a broader understanding of the situation. It is their experience that is a significant factor in enabling pastoral heads in secondary schools to quickly 'get to the bottom' of certain situations.

A vast range of information is received by teachers, on education-related matters, from a wide range of sources. There is a multitude of policy documents, regulations, laws, advice and anecdotes produced concerning all aspects of education. This is published in books, newspapers and on the World Wide Web. There are programmes both fictional and factual on television and radio. There is soon to be a whole new government-funded digital teachers' television channel in the UK – no other profession can boast a whole channel devoted to their needs! Teachers are used to evaluating and then using, storing or disregarding all information presented to them. Academic or formal research has, though, come to be seen as something that others (usually very learned or expertly trained) do and as having little practical application in the classroom (McNamara, 2002). Thus many teachers do not acknowledge the potential of a more formal, structured approach to research in their professional lives.

This book suggests that we are all researchers and that it is vital for professionals to develop a critical approach to their work. For this reason we must embrace the many forms that the research process can take. That includes more formal research as well as the more informal and routine daily information processing that takes place.

■ ■ ■ Formal research

What does the term 'research' mean when used in relation to the study of education? Anderson (1998: 6) explains that 'Research in education is a disciplined attempt to address or solve problems through the collection and analysis of primary data for the purpose of description, explanation, generalisation and prediction'. Blaxter et al. (2001: 5) counsel that 'All types of research should be "planned, cautious, systematic, and reliable ways of finding out or deepening understanding"'. Definitions abound but the use of such words as 'disciplined', 'systematic' and 'cautious' in these two quotes is characteristic of most because, for researchers, the rigour of their approach is paramount.

Verma and Mallick (1999) suggest that research has attained a high degree of respectability and that educators, politicians, business people and others turn to researchers when seeking information on which to base decisions. Most advanced societies have evolved a research-oriented culture, or are in the process of moving in that direction. Formal research, then, would appear to be the systematic gathering, presenting and analysing of data. Actually, some research is more systematic than others. Some research is more formalized than others. The process can appear mysterious to 'outsiders', making researchers seem special and somehow different. It is important to 'demystify' the process in the rest of this chapter since we are all players of the research game.

Academic research essentially refines the information-gathering practices of daily living. Watching other people becomes observation, asking questions becomes interviewing. If the questions are written down they are called questionnaires. The difference is that these information-gathering practices are carried out in a more conscious manner. They become more structured, rigorous and deliberate. The findings are recorded systematically and with care. The research methods are formalized for a number of possible motives: to make more 'scientific', to make larger scale, to make more authoritative, to 'prove', to inform action, to take further than individual experiences. Research, however complex or formally presented, is simply a part of the process of finding out and understanding phenomena.

■ ■ ■ Purposes of research

Clough and Nutbrown (2002) explain that all social research is persuasive, purposive, positional and political and these are the reasons why it is conducted. The need to persuade someone or a group of people about something underlies all research whether it is persuading customers to buy a particular product or persuading teachers of a particular teaching method. Looking back to Anderson's definition we can see that research is purposive in that it attempts to produce something such as the solution to a problem. Research is positional because it is imbued with the perspective of the researcher and the research funders and is derived from a set of circumstances where a problem was defined necessarily from a particular viewpoint or position. As Clough and Nutbrown (2002: 10) observe: 'Research which did not express a more or less distinct perspective on the world would not be research at all; it would have the status of a telephone directory where data are listed without analysis'.

Finally, research is political because it seeks to make a difference within a policy context. Practitioner researchers, for instance, may seek to change the behaviour policy of a school based on research they have conducted into the efficiency of sanctions.

■ ■ ■ Types of research

We can never dissociate the motives for and context of our research from the types of research methodologies we employ. There are a great many types of research defined either by their context, for example, market research, or by their approach. Verma and Mallick (1999: 11) developed the following typology of research which highlights 'critical differences between research that is oriented to the development of theory and that designed to deal with practical problems'.

- *Pure or basic research.* Concerned with the development of theory and discovery of fundamental facts to extend the boundaries of knowledge.

- *Applied or field research.* The application of new knowledge to everyday problems. Though more practical it usually employs the same rigorous methodology as pure research.

- *Action research*. Research into specific practical situations carried out by practitioners to solve clearly identified problems in order to improve them. As such it is continuous and cyclical. (Action research is discussed in more detail in the following chapter.)

- *Evaluation research*. This is carried out to assess the effectiveness of specific projects to see if the original aims have been achieved. Many government-funded projects allocate a proportion of their budgets for evaluation.

Hammersley (2002) suggests a distinction between what he terms as *scientific* and *practical* research. The criteria of validity and relevance are important to both types of research but are given different weight and interpreted differently within each. Hammersley further divides scientific enquiry into *theoretical scientific research* and *substantive scientific research*. Practical research subdivides into *dedicated practical research* the goal of which is to provide information to a specific group, *democratic practical research* that provides information for anyone interested in a particular issue, *contract-based practical research* where the project is commissioned to produce information on a specific issue, and *autonomous practical research* when researchers are autonomous in how they approach an issue of interest.

Both Hammersley and Verma and Mallick's typologies highlight the key point that there are different types of research with different purposes. Each have particular strengths and weaknesses and, whilst these types of research are complementary to each other, 'criticism arises, in part at least, from the impossibility of satisfying, simultaneously, all the criteria by which research findings can be judged' (Hammersley, 2002: 124).

■ ■ ■ Approaches to classroom research

The way in which information is collected, the valuing of certain forms of data over others and the analysis and presentation of findings, are all significant parts of the research process that affect how a classroom is portrayed. Through a discussion of research paradigms, we consider fundamental beliefs underpinning the research process and how these frame the ways in which we understand the world around us. The implications of this are extrapolated in relation to practitioner research.

There are different ways that we can consider what is happening in schools and classrooms. One approach involves a search to identify the key factors influencing outcomes so that they can then be applied generally in the quest to raise educational standards. An important part of this approach is to measure performance. Thus there is particular interest here in pupil attainment scores, attendance figures, delinquency rates and the variables that affect these. Central to this approach is the establishment of the cause and effect relationships that operate within education. An alternative approach seeks to explain what is happening in schools and classrooms using the perspectives of those involved: pupils, teachers, teaching assistants. The aim here is to 'understand' more fully the complexities of school life and the nature of teaching and learning. There is a concern with feelings and perceptions and an admitting of different perspectives that render objectification or quantification redundant. These are two approaches to understanding what is happening in classrooms and they clearly reflect alternative ideologies or views about the value and purposes of education (see Bartlett et al., 2001, for a discussion of ideologies). However, whilst they are different, it is also possible to see how in some ways they are complementary since important elements within each approach are of value. These different ideologies of education have corresponding alternative beliefs concerning how research is carried out. This brings us to consider research paradigms.

■ ■ ■ What are research paradigms?

This term describes models of research that reflect general agreement on the nature of the world and how to investigate it. Within a paradigm there would be a general consensus on the research methods that are appropriate and acceptable for gathering data and also those which are not, or are at least less, acceptable. A paradigm then: 'is a network of coherent ideas about the nature of the world and of the functions of researchers which, adhered to by a group of researchers, conditions the patterns of their thinking and underpins their research actions' (Bassey, 1990: 41).

In the social sciences research is often divided into two major paradigms, the positivist or quantitative and the interpretivist or qualitative. These are perhaps best seen as characteristics clustering into two general groups rather than as clear extremes.

■ ■ ■ Positivist paradigm

The positivist paradigm developed in the nineteenth century in the wake of the apparent success of the natural, or physical, sciences in advancing understanding of the world. People's lives had been significantly improved by scientific advances in particular, their health and living standards (see Hitchcock and Hughes, 1995).

The positivist or scientific approach consists of testing a hypothesis (initial idea, unproved theory) via experiments. This often involves having two identical groups, a control group to which nothing is done and all factors which could affect it (variables) are kept constant. The other group, the experimental group, is subject to some change in conditions (certain specific variables are altered in a controlled way). In this way, any resulting difference between the experimental and the control group is deemed to be due to the change in the variables made by the scientist in the experiment. Experiments are able to establish cause and effect relationships. Altering a particular variable has a particular, measurable effect.

Experiments in the natural sciences are said to be objective, producing findings that are unaffected by the opinions and hopes of the researcher. The outcome of the experiment, if carried out under the same conditions, will always be consistent. Thus natural science is systematic, experiments are replicable, the results are documented and knowledge of the natural world is incremental (see Cohen et al., 2000; Yates, 2004). Research in the natural sciences thus has high prestige and the findings are treated with respect. Pure research in the natural sciences also became over the years a focus for applied research with the potential to inform future policy. Such a status was regarded as desirable by those interested in the social world and thus an interest grew in developing the social sciences.

The positivist belief is that the approach of the natural sciences could be applied to the social world. It assumes that the social world exists in the same way as does the natural world (Yates, 2004). Individual behaviour is influenced by various pressures, internal such as biological and psychological pressures, and/or external pressures, such as the norms and values held by the social groups to which we belong. As a result regular and predictable patterns of behaviour can be said to be displayed by individuals and groups in society, creating social forces in the form of both external and internalized constraints. Individuals operate within these internalized constraints and influences which derive from interaction with the wider society.

Positivists believe that the structures that create the apparent order in social life can be discovered by research. They contend that society can be investigated in the same objective way as the natural world. The approach is empirical in that it shows something exists through observations, that is, data. Going beyond theory and debate, positivist researchers attempt to show that what is being discussed in the theories actually exists because it has the status of the external, it is not just hypothetical. The purpose is to uncover the 'social facts' which make up our world (see the work of Durkheim, 1964; 1970).

To be objective, the positivist social science researcher would ideally like to conduct experiments in the same way as the natural scientist. Some educational research is able to use this method, for instance, certain psychological experiments (see Chapter 7 for a discussion of the experimental method in educational research). However for much social research it is not possible to create experimental and control groups and to alter variables in a controlled way. People need to be studied in their usual environment if they are to act 'naturally'. Much of the seminal work of the Swiss psychologist, Piaget, was based on experiments conducted with his own children in 'laboratory' conditions which have since been criticized for their inappropriateness. There are also moral objections to treating people in certain ways, so although it might appear to be interesting to deprive babies of human affection and see how their personalities develop, it certainly would not be ethical to do so!

In order to show relationships between variables, researchers frequently use the comparative method. This is where groups are compared and differences are noted. The purpose is to identify significant variables which explain the differences between the groups. The aim ultimately is to show cause and effect relationships. This strategy is felt to be more reliable the greater the numbers used in the comparison. For positivists size does matter. Also important is the sample's representativeness of the whole population. The findings take on greater significance when the data set is larger and can be categorized and compared in a number of ways. It is important that the researcher maintains an objective standpoint and keeps personal 'contamination' of the data collection process to a minimum. The most effective positivist research is able to be replicated by others, as with experiments in the natural sciences, or at least compared closely with other similar studies. For these reasons positivist researchers prefer structured methods of data collection which can be carried out on a large scale (macro studies). The data favoured is quantitative, usually presented as statistical tables, enabling others to see how the data has been interpreted and allowing for more accurate comparisons. The aim is to be able to generalize from the findings.

Certain criticisms have been levelled at the positivist paradigm and the use of statistics in social science research:

1. Statistics indicate trends but do not explain why people have done or said certain things. Since they do not yield detailed accounts of people's reasons, the meanings obtained from statistical data remain superficial. Statistics of truancy, absence or examination success may show interesting patterns but it is the stories behind them that explain these trends. In this way statistics may be seen as impersonal. Positivist methods may ignore the richness of detailed individual accounts.

2. Statistical correlations should not be confused with causality. We could discern a correlation between the levels of umbrella-carrying and car wiper-blades operating but they are not causally linked; rather, both are consequent upon rainfall levels. A facetious example perhaps but similarly there may be statistical relations between social deprivation and lack of educational success so we need to go further than statistical analysis to see if the link is meaningful and to seek explanations.

3. Statistical tables and analysis may appear to be objective but the choices researchers make in their compilations must not be overlooked. A researcher decides what to look for, asks certain questions yet ignores others, and collects, collates, interprets and categorizes the data. There appears little likelihood of the whole process being unaffected by human contamination (see Cohen et al., 2000). Consider the construction of performance tables and how the data can be compiled in different ways to give very different impressions. Edwards and Usher (2000) provide strong theoretical grounds for challenging the objectivity and scientific claims of positivist approaches to education research.

■ ■ ■ Interpretivist paradigm

This paradigm embraces many social perspectives, notably phenomenology, symbolic interactionism, ethnomethodology (see Cohen et al., 2000, or Flick, 2002, for a discussion of these). Interpretivism does not view society as having a fixed structure, hidden or otherwise because the social world is created by the interactions of individuals. Norms and values exist but as shifting organic elements of social life. They are used and changed by people as they interpret and respond to events. There are external pressures upon individuals but they do not act as some sort of external system controlling people. Weber (see Cuff and Payne, 1984) maintained that actions must be seen as meaningful at the level of inter-action. By this he meant that action is taken to be deliberate and meaningful to those involved and the interpretivist paradigm seeks to understand the meanings behind these actions.

The interpretivist tries to show how choices are made by participants or 'actors' in social situations within the process of interaction. For the interpretivist there is no one objective reality that exists outside the actor's explanations, just different versions of events. Pupils, the classroom teacher, other teachers at the school, parents, all have a view of what goes on and act according to how they interpret events. The researcher in this paradigm seeks to 'understand' these actions.

Interpretivists prefer more 'naturalistic' forms of data collection, making use of individual accounts and biographies and often including detailed descriptions to give a 'feeling' for the environment. Methods favoured in interpretivist studies are informal interviews and observations which allow the situation to be as 'normal' as possible (Hitchcock and Hughes, 1995). These methods are often reliant upon the ability of the researcher to be reflexive in the research process. Interpretivist studies tend to be small scale (micro), aiming for detail and understanding rather than statistical representativeness. Whilst it is not possible to generalize from such studies, researchers in this paradigm do attempt to be as rigorous as possible.

Woods (1999: 2) suggests that qualitative research focuses on natural settings and is 'concerned with life as it is lived, things as they happen, situations as they are constructed in the day-to-day, moment-to-moment course of events'. The researcher seeks to understand and to portray the participants' perceptions and understandings of the particular situation or event. Interaction is ongoing and there is a continuing chain of events which gives insight into how people live and the research emphasizes this process. Woods (1999) also cites the important part played by inductive analysis and grounded theory in qualitative research. The term 'grounded theory' comes from the work of Glaser and Strauss (1967) who suggested that in qualitative studies the researchers do not begin hoping to prove or disprove a set hypothesis. They may have ideas on how 'things will go' but the theory comes from the data they have collected after the research has begun. It is 'grounded' in the data and the experiences of the researcher rather than being imposed upon the research before commencement.

In summary, Yates (2004: 138) says that qualitative research attempts to do one or more of the following:

- achieve an in-depth understanding and detailed description of a particular aspect of an individual, a case history or a group's experience(s)

- explore how individuals or group members give meaning to and express their understanding of themselves, their experiences and/or their worlds

- find out and describe in detail social events and to explore why they are happening, rather than how often

- explore the complexity, ambiguity and specific detailed processes taking place in a social context.

We can see that the qualitative methods used in social science research are readily applicable in the context of many practitioner researchers.

Ethnography

This is a research strategy sometimes adopted by interpretivists which developed from anthropological studies of small-scale societies. Scott (1996) suggests that the spread of this approach can be seen as a reaction to the dominance of positivism in social science. Ethnography is characterized by 'thick' descriptive accounts of the activities of particular groups studied. Accounts focus on the micro, spending much time looking at small groups and particular institutions.

For Walford (2001), ethnography takes into account the wider cultural context in which individuals or groups exist and live, as part of seeking to understand their behaviour and values. Fieldwork takes numerous forms and researchers gather data from many sources, with particular reliance on 'naturalistic' interpretive methods such as participant observation and informal interviews. This is to develop a multidimensional appreciation of these cultures and individuals. The researcher must have a long-term engagement with the situation to observe developments at first hand and to experience the culture. Paradoxically, the researcher should also attempt to view cultures dispassionately and to step outside their situation at times; what has been termed as viewing situations as 'anthropologically strange' (see Hammersley and Atkinson, 1995). Thus Walford (2001) sees ethnographic researchers developing their theoretical accounts over time as they conduct their ethnography. The aim is to construct an account that gives a deep and rich appreciation of the people who have been studied. Central to the description and analysis in ethnography are the views and perceptions of the actors.

This research strategy then, studies groups and individuals in their natural settings, considers the perspectives of those involved and the culture they are living in, uses a wide range of methods to develop a deep understanding and produces accounts which both actors and researchers recognize. It therefore has much to offer practitioner researchers in education. McNally et al. (2003: 6) explain that they plan to use an ethnographic approach to their study of early professional learning because 'a deep understanding of the nature of EPL requires sustained contact with the learners and their context. Immersion in these contexts is perhaps best achieved by the deployment of teacher researchers, trained and supported as case study ethnographers of new teachers in their own schools'.

Teachers as researchers are part of the classroom situation, they are aware of the complex social interaction that takes place. Much of what they are interested in studying, concerning pupil learning and development, needs to be understood in the context of daily classroom life and this, in turn, must be part of any explanation. Teachers are also in a position to gather data over a long period and often look to a variety of sources such as brief observations, snatched chats, as well as the more structured observations and interviews. They keep records of pupils, mark their work, speak with them as individuals and groups. They have teaching assistants and teacher colleagues who may also gather data. There is the opportunity to photograph, video-record and tape-record. Most significantly, teachers are aware that the quality of data gathered is a reflection of the relationship and understanding between the pupils and the researcher. This understanding is a key part of the ethnographic research approach.

Inevitably there are criticisms of qualitative research and we have seen earlier how these found particular expression within a policy context intent on 'driving up standards'. Policy-makers felt that interpretivist approaches failed to provide clear-cut solutions, presenting instead an overly complex analysis of educational issues (Nisbet, 2000, cited in Greenbank, 2003).

Approaches to the research process and the type of data considered acceptable very much depend upon how those carrying out the research see the world. Much falls within and between the two paradigms of positivism and interpretivism but sometimes this dichotomy proves to be rather too simplistic ignoring a multitude of variations. Several proponents of action research suggest that this two-paradigm view of research emanates from a traditional academic approach and they are critical of its application to professionally based research. McNiff (2002), for instance, suggests critical theoretical and living theory approaches as being more appropriate. Clough and Nutbrown (2002) suggest that research studies often move between these paradigms selecting the most appropriate for different parts of the study. They suggest that 'The issue is not so much a question of which paradigm to work within but how to dissolve that distinction in the interests of developing research design which serves the investigation of the questions posed through that research' (2002: 19).

Much practitioner research borrows from both major paradigms using quantitative and/or qualitative methods as appropriate. Sometimes clear measures can be used and there will be a search for 'proof' whilst in other instances there is a need for interpretation and description that acknowledge the relativity of social life. It is certainly the case that whilst performance indicators are still used in education, for many practitioners, much of what they see as the most important aspects of their work cannot be measured in quantitative terms. Thus it is important for practitioner researchers to recognize the relevance of research paradigms in shaping how their projects are designed and conducted. This understanding could also help them to design imaginative research projects using a more eclectic approach.

■ ■ ■ Important research concepts

In undertaking a research project we need to consider some fundamental concepts that are of great significance in any piece of research. Thus we now turn to a discussion of the importance of reliability and validity in practitioner research. Triangulation is outlined as a significant strategy that can be applied in order to increase the validity of the findings.

Reliability

Reliability describes the extent to which a research instrument or method is repeatable. It is an assessment of the consistency of any method. Thus for Pole and Lampard (2002) the reliability of a measure is the extent to which respondents will consistently respond to it in the same way. Corbetta (2003: 81) says that reliability marks: 'The degree to which a given procedure for transforming a concept into a variable produces the same results in tests repeated with the same empirical tools (stability) or equivalent ones (equivalence).' In other words the more reliable the method of data collection the more likely it is to give similar results in subsequent administrations. An unreliable measure will yield different results every time it is administered (Anderson, 1998).

Positivist researchers who wish to carry out large-scale research are most concerned with reliability. The methods need to be capable of being applied to large numbers of respondents in order to generate the data required. To be able to make the desired statistical comparisons the collection of data needs to be consistent, that is, reliable. In contrast, the interpretivist researcher is likely to be more concerned with the suitability of the methods for eliciting qualitative, accurate and detailed accounts from each respondent. Thus the emphasis on reliability varies according to the paradigm of the researcher.

It should be noted that a high level of reliability of a data collection instrument does not necessarily mean that it is accurate. For instance, if a tutor asks students to evaluate the course by named questionnaire and they are aware that the tutor will shortly be marking their assignments, this is likely to concentrate their minds. Not surprisingly, the tutor will have positive student feedback. Whilst this method can be said to be reliable, in that its questions are similarly understood by successive cohorts of students and thus it is always measuring the same thing, its accuracy in terms of the truthfulness of the student responses is certainly suspect.

Validity

Validity and its measurement plays an important part in determining the appropriate methodology to employ. Validity refers to the 'truthfulness', 'correctness' or accuracy of research data. If results are to be considered accurate, then the research instrument must measure what we claim it to measure. Thus 'an indicator is valid to the extent that it empirically represents the concept it purports to measure' (Punch 1998: 100). For instance, tests of mathematical ability might actually be producing results which are indicative of the ability to read the questions rather than of mathematical prowess. If our methods are at fault, then the findings will be invalid and the research worthless. In aiming to increase validity, positivists emphasize the standardization of data collection whilst using as large a sample as possible. Thus the piloting of any method for accuracy is very important.

Another approach to validity, more associated with an interpretivist approach, places emphasis on the final account and how the researcher is able to defend the interpretations they make from the data (Punch, 1998). In other words, the researcher needs to show on what evidence they base their findings. This can be done in a number of ways such as giving full explanations as to how data were gathered, member checks (Maykut and Morehouse, 1994) whereby research participants are asked if their accounts have been recorded accurately, or reducing researcher bias by giving a colleague samples of all data collected to verify the analysis and conclusions drawn by the researcher (as suggested by Miles and Huberman, 1994). In action research the openness of the findings to scrutiny and discussion by fellow practitioners is seen as a significant means of ensuring the validity of what is often small-scale research carried out by researchers who are themselves part of the research project (McNiff, 2002).

Triangulation

Triangulation is a navigational term which means to fix one's position from two known bearings. This process is carried out by researchers to increase the validity of their research and it means checking one's findings by using several points of reference. In effect, the researcher is approaching the object of the research from as many different angles and perspectives as possible in order to gain a greater understanding. Researchers can triangulate by using a number of different fieldworkers in the collection and analysis of data; seeking the contribution of varied groups of respondents such as pupils, teachers and parents; using a range of research methods; considering qualitative and quantitative data and so on. Miles and Huberman (1994) pointed to triangulation as a way of life. If findings were consciously checked and double-checked using different sources of evidence then verification would be built in 'by seeing or hearing multiple instances of it from different sources, by using different methods and by squaring the finding with others it needs to be squared with' (1994: 267).

The positivist would hope to show congruency of results from triangulation. The interpretivist would use the different sources of data to give greater depth to their analysis, corroborating or leading to discussion of variation in the findings (Woods, 1999). Thus for Hammersley and Atkinson (1995: 232): 'What is involved in triangulation is not the combination of different kinds of data per se, but rather an attempt to relate different sorts of data in such a way as to counteract various possible threats to the validity of our analysis.' Certainly both paradigms would suggest the use of triangulation to increase the validity of their findings but would use it in slightly different ways. In order to produce a more thorough and rigorous piece of research, several research methods are often used in conjunction with one another. The main methods, in fact, often complement each other. For instance, what has been seen during observations can be raised in interviews by the researcher. This will give an understanding of why something happened as well as a descriptive account. Triangulation is likely to appear as almost a natural process to practitioners who are used to considering different viewpoints and obtaining data from several sources in order more fully to understand particular incidents or aspects of their daily work.

■ ■ ■ Research ethics

Though this is a short section of this book, it is nevertheless very important. There are always ethical considerations that must be addressed before embarking upon a research project and taken into account whilst the project is ongoing. It is well worth any prospective researcher consulting the *Ethical Guidelines for Educational Research* produced by the British Educational Research Association (BERA, 2003a).

In suggesting 'that all educational research should be conducted within an ethic of respect for:

- the person;
- knowledge;
- democratic values; and
- the quality of educational research' (BERA, 2003a: 3).

BERA sets out guidelines concerning the researcher's responsibilities to participants in the research, to sponsors of research and to the wider community of educational researchers. For practising teacher researchers certain ethical points can be extrapolated from these guidelines as follows:

1. *Consent of those involved.* Consent from the school management and any colleagues involved should be sought before the research takes place. It may also be appropriate to seek the consent of others, such as parents and pupils. Whilst teachers continually monitor and make professional judgements on the pupils they teach, how much the pupils should know of, and actually be involved in, the research needs to be considered. Certainly it would be worth discussing the research and any findings with pupils at some point even if it is only to reflect upon any changes or developments that have resulted, such as how their work has improved, how the organization of the classroom has changed and so on.

2. *Honesty and openness.* Whilst not wishing to influence the behaviour of the respondents, the researcher needs to consider how open they make the research process. Deception can certainly prove to be counter-productive in the long term as well as being morally objectionable. Much of the classroom research carried out

by teachers actually benefits from being open and involving others.

3. *Access to findings.* It is an important principle that any final report or submission of findings is presented to the respondents or is at least made accessible to them. Seeking confirmation from respondents is certainly a part of the validation process for many of the methods discussed in this volume. As well as strengthening the validity of the findings, feedback from those involved is often an important part of the action research cycle.

4. *Possible effects of the research on participants.* The effects of carrying out the research on those involved needs to be considered in terms of both the actual research process and the future actions that may result from the findings. This lends further support to the need to be as open as possible in the research process and to alert the respondents to any possible effects.

5. *Anonymity of those involved.* The anonymity of those taking part in the research should be ensured by the researcher and the confidentiality of data collected guaranteed.

An interesting example of an ethical issue affecting a research proposal is highlighted in the following case. A teacher had access to a very sophisticated information technology (IT) package that appeared to have great potential for developing the literacy, IT capabilities and communication skills of Key Stage 1 (KS1) children. This was also a package that the teacher felt sure the pupils would find enjoyable and would therefore also have long-term motivational benefits. There were two parallel classes in Year 1 at the school, and the teacher was proposing to run the package with one of the classes as part of their literacy programme. This would constitute the experimental group and the academic development of its pupil members would be closely monitored. The second class was to be taught literacy using the traditional format and was not to have the use of the IT package. The performance of this group was also to be monitored and the pupils would act as a comparison or control group.

The concerns that are raised in this example are around the targeting of school resources for the benefit of one class of pupils and not the other. The control group is likely, quite reasonably, to feel discriminated against. How would parents of children in the control class in particular react to pupils being treated so differently? They may feel that their children were being deprived of educational opportunities. It would seem inexcusable for the parents not to be told of such research and, if not officially informed, the consequences of them finding out unofficially would be very damaging.

This example shows the ethical questions that can confound the use of experimental and control groups in education research. In this example the research had the worthy aim of examining the effects of an IT package. However, it could have been designed in such a way that pupils were not split into distinct experimental and control groups since this was such a desirable facility. Pupil use of the package could have been evaluated on a more individual basis and each child's progress monitored.

Those working and researching in fields such as education, social work and medicine are continually presented with ethical dilemmas. For instance, discovering through interviews information concerning the drug use, sexual activity or other deviant behaviour of pupils has always presented the researcher/teacher with the dilemma of whether to protect confidential sources or to report such activity to parents and the 'authorities'. It is important that all researchers take an ethical stance in their research and only act in a way that they can morally justify even though this may not always be easy (see Oliver, 2003, for a discussion of this).

■ ■ ■ Conclusion

This chapter has provided a brief overview of some fundamental research approaches and constructs, defining in broad terms the main forms of educational research and outlining the major research paradigms. We have looked briefly at some of the key concepts informing the development of research studies and sought to demonstrate the critical importance of ethical considerations. There are many authoritative research texts that provide a far deeper level of discussion than is attempted here, see, for instance, Cohen et al. (2000). We have established through this discussion that, although much practitioner research is classroom based, a wider view of the research process and the perspectives that inform it are highly relevant if practitioners are to design credible studies. In the next chapter we discuss the genesis of the idea of teachers as researchers.

■ ■ ■ Task: Using different paradigms

1. Take one of the following research topics and consider, first, how a positivist and then an interpretivist researcher would approach it. Consider what each would be looking for in their research, the type of data they would collect, what would be considered appropriate methods and who the possible respondents would be. Research topics to consider: pupil truancy, pupil transition from primary to secondary school, bullying, assessment at the end of a particular key stage. Please add any other topic that you think may be interesting.

2. Note similarities and differences between the likely approaches of the two paradigms, and the effects of these upon the resulting research.

■ ■ ■ Suggested further reading

Clough, P. and Nutbrown, C. (2002) *A Student's Guide to Methodology.* London: Sage.

This text helps the reader to develop an understanding of the research process through a series of challenging activities that the authors have developed through their teaching. It encourages the novice researcher to seriously consider the nature of research from different perspectives.

Cohen, L., Manion, L. and Morrison, K. (2000) *Research Methods in Education.* 5th edn. London: RoutledgeFalmer.

This is a research text written specifically for students on undergraduate and post-graduate courses. The authors cover the whole research process and include useful sections on ethics, validity and reliability.

Hammersley, M. (2002) *Educational Research, Policymaking and Practice.* London: Paul Chapman Publishing.

This is an interesting text for the more experienced practitioner researcher, being written primarily for masters and doctoral level courses. It considers the complex relationship between research, practice and policy and presents a useful typology for varieties of research.

Oliver, P. (2003) *The Student's Guide to Research Ethics*. Maidenhead: Open University Press.

This text introduces the reader to ethical issues that occur in research. It considers every stage of the research process from design to writing the final report. This is a very accessible volume that covers an area that must be addressed by all researchers.

Yates, S. (2004) *Doing Social Science Research*. London: Sage/Open University Press.

This book is useful for those new to the research process. Written as a general text for social science students, it provides an introductory overview of the research process. It offers a clear explanation of the main research paradigms and their associated methodologies. Many interesting readings are used as illustrative examples.

■ ■ ■ Chapter 3

Teachers as reflective practitioners

■ ■ ■ Introduction

This chapter outlines the history of action research in education out of which the notion of teachers as researchers evolved. Political pressures in education throughout the 1980s and 1990s, whilst restricting the autonomy of teachers, also adversely affected the development of action research. The growth of school effectiveness and school improvement research is briefly outlined in the chapter and, in the light of this discussion, the meaning and nature of practitioner research are then considered.

■ ■ ■ The development of action research

Teachers, in common with similar professional occupations, have a history of researching into their own practice. The current promotion of practitioner research by the Teacher Training Agency and the Department for Education and Skills (DfES), however, seems to make little or no reference to this tradition. A brief examination of the development of teachers as action researchers may reveal why.

The development of action research is often attributed to the work of Kurt Lewin (1946) who was seeking ways of increasing productivity in industry by involving a larger proportion of the workforce in decision-making. He also saw what became termed the 'action research approach' as a way of tackling many of the post-Second World War social problems. He developed a spiral of action that involved fact-finding, planning and implementation. This act of professionals conducting research in order to solve professional problems could be readily applied to many areas, education being a prime example.

The action research 'movement' in education in Britain has been greatly influenced by the work of Lawrence Stenhouse at the Schools' Council (1967–72). The Schools' Council was the forerunner of various government curriculum agencies but, unlike the subsequent National Curriculum Council and the Qualifications and Curriculum Agency, Schools' Council members were drawn from academics, educationalists and teachers. Stenhouse felt that teachers needed to be at the centre of curriculum development if it was to be effective. Therefore it was essential that teachers reflected upon practice, shared experiences and evaluated their work if the education of pupils was to improve. For Stenhouse, each classroom could be seen as a laboratory and each teacher a member of a research community.

Stenhouse found the 'objectives model' of curriculum design to be uneducational as it assumed knowledge as a given and discouraged wider questioning and individual development whilst encouraging passive acceptance of the facts as presented. For teachers to appear authoritative and to present subject content as beyond doubt was a misrepresentation encouraged by many in education. He viewed knowledge and its structure as inherently problematic and contestable. For this reason Stenhouse favoured a process model of curriculum design that was based upon learners questioning and exploring in order to gain their own understanding. Teachers themselves, whilst having knowledge about what they are teaching, are cast in the role of learners alongside their students. For Stenhouse it was this continual questioning and learning by teachers that gave them more to offer their students. In this way learning itself is a research process and research is seen as the basis for teaching (Stenhouse, 1983).

Stenhouse believed in the professional desire of teachers to improve education for their pupils and so benefit society. For this reason he considered teachers the best judges of teaching. By working in research communities they would be able to reflect upon and then improve their practice. Other interested members of the community, such as parents and employers, would in turn, be drawn into this research process. In this way a social democratic ideology ran through the work of the Schools' Council. Curriculum reform was visualized as happening at the grass-roots level and involving all those with a stake in education. Action resulting from the reflective process was regarded as a means of empowering practitioners and, therefore, central to the professional development of teachers. It is noteworthy that an abhorrence of the notion of empowering teachers and viewing them as education experts was what led to the eventual demise of the Schools' Council under the Conservative government of Margaret Thatcher.

This development of action research fitted Schön's (1983) view of the reflective practitioner where discussion of practice is shared both with clients and colleagues. Resulting from this, modern professional communities reflect upon, discuss and learn from each other's work. It also ties in with Hoyle's (1980) view of extended professionals who were likely to be involved in action research as a 'natural' part of their professional development.

Action research grew in part out of disillusionment with traditional forms of educational research that were conducted by the universities during the 1960s and 1970s. These were felt to adopt an academic approach to research and to be of little practical use to those working in classrooms. They took a disengaged stance and offered no help in terms of the practice of teaching. Also, much influential academic research of the time had promoted a view that either innate factors (Jensen, 1973) or wider social circumstances (Douglas, 1964) largely determined overall educational achievement. It was as though schools did not make a difference to pupil attainment and it was the influence of wider social forces on the pupil or natural ability that were seen as the key factors. If anything, schools only reinforced these existing inequalities acting as processing agencies in which teachers were unwitting players (Bowles and Gintis, 1976). Such research gave little encouragement to teachers about how to change or improve things.

Though closely linked with higher education institutions that provided mentors who were a valuable source of support, action research was seen as a new approach to research carried out by professionals. It was thus rooted in practice and moved away from the traditional academic approach based upon the major research paradigms. McNiff (1988) spoke of a wish to create a study of education that was grounded in practice and developed by those involved. Thus teachers were to develop their research skills to evaluate their practice. The process needed to be rigorous and critical if it was to create effective change. Injunctions to become more critical meant far more than simply evaluating practice for many proponents of action research (Carr and Kemmis, 1986). The development of critical theory was seen as a questioning of the whole purpose and techniques employed by teachers. It involved asking fundamental questions about why things are done in a certain way and why other processes are not used. This would encourage further research, experimentation and, ultimately, change. There would be a linking of theory and practice alongside the development of research for action.

■ ■ ■ Defining action research

According to Elliott, a lifelong proponent, action research is 'the study of a social situation with a view to improving the quality of action within it' (1991: 69), and 'theorising from the standpoint of action in order to act with "understanding" of the practical situation' (2003: 172). Altrichter et al. (1993) suggest that action research starts from practical questions that fit in with the working conditions of the teachers. Methods of data collection are tailored to suit the circumstances. Each research project is designed for a specific set of circumstances and so is unique.

These definitions indicate that action research starts with a problem, issue or set of questions arising out of professional concerns. Initial research is carried out to collect data that clarifies the situation. A plan of action is devised in the light of this evidence. This is put into place and the effects carefully monitored. This is likely to lead to further refined questions and so further developments which will, in turn, be implemented and researched. However, what is critical for Elliott (2003) is that the action part of improving practice is an integral part of the teacher's construction of new knowledge and understanding of the problem. The action research process has frequently been shown in diagrammatic form as some form of developmental spiral.

Action research is curriculum development at the classroom level. It is concerned with how to improve education practice and it is practitioners themselves who carry out the research in examining and developing their teaching. The nature of this form of practitioner research means that it is carried out in the teacher's own place of work and so the case study approach is the most common. Ideally, an eclectic view of data collection is taken, with the researcher using a variety of methods to examine the particular issue. The process whereby researchers are able to use their own understandings to interpret the situations they are investigating is termed *reflexivity*. This is an important aspect of action research

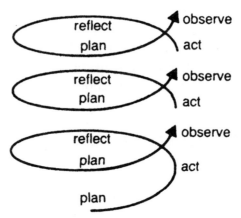

■ **Figure 3.1**
McNiff's original action research spiral (McNiff, J. with Whitehead, J. (2002) Action Research: Principles and Practice. London: RoutledgeFalmer.)

and it is expected that the reflexivity of the researchers will be height-ened as they develop their research skills.

Increased validity is aimed at through a rigorous approach to the research coupled with triangulation and openness at all stages of the process. Though it is not possible to generalize from the findings of such small-scale research, its strength, according to Bassey (1998), lies in its transferability to similar situations. Evans et al. (2000) explain this as applying ideas in other classrooms and institutions and adapting them to the new context. Validity is also strengthened as communities of researchers in schools examine and discuss each other's findings, an activity described by Elliott (1993) as 'discoursive consciousness'. This process would involve others and develop a wider understanding of the nature of education as part of the social democratic process. Kemmis and Wilkinson (1998) also stress the participatory nature of action research. They see action research itself as a social and educational process that is part of the development of a professional community.

■ ■ ■ Criticisms of action research

The use of diagrams showing action research as a continuous process of development has been criticized as inadvertently promoting a rigid approach to research (Carter and Halsall, 1998). Dadds, for instance, realized that 'the tidy action research cycle was never that tidy in the practices of research' (Dadds and Hart, 2001: 7). Diagrams that indicate stages in a research cycle may encourage the view that these are the 'correct' order in which to conduct action research. This may create problems when any new researcher finds that they are deviating from these proscribed stages. The diagrams themselves may appear daunting and even confusing to the novice (Hopkins, 2002). In fairness, many of those who designed action research diagrams, such as Elliott (1991), only intended them to be used as guides that were not proscriptive in any way. More recently McNiff (2002) has developed her original model, which she accepts could be seen as rather prescriptive, to now show how the action research process can take many turns (Figure 3.2).

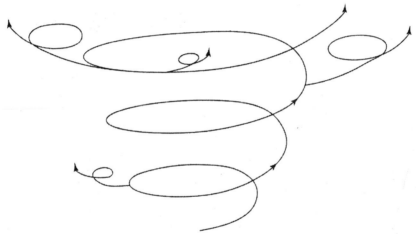

▨ **Figure 3.2**
McNiff's latest representation of the action research process ((McNiff, J. with White-head, J. (2002) Action Research: Principles and Practice. London: RoutledgeFalmer.))

Those who adopt an action research approach have also been criticized for assuming that research begins with what might appear a management issue, a premise that something is wrong that needs to be fixed or made better. However, many teachers may be interested, initially, in developing a broader understanding of the learning process rather than investigating problems. For these reasons Hopkins (2002: 51) prefers to use the phrase 'classroom research by teachers' and Carter and Halsall (1998) 'teacher research' rather than action research.

■ ■ ■ Action research at the end of the twentieth century

There have always been different interpretations of what action research actually involves (Bryant, 1996). For many of the proponents of the late 1970s and early 1980s it provided a whole philosophy of the future development and control of education linked to the social democratic movement in the wider society. Thus according to Carr and Kemmis:

> it comes out on the side of the control of education by self-critical communities of researchers, including teachers, students, parents, educational administrators and others. Creating the conditions under which these participants can take collaborative responsibility for the development and reform of education is the task of a critical educational science. Educational action research offers a means by which this can be achieved. (1986: 211)

An evangelical approach to action research that sees it as a quest for personal and professional fulfilment can still be seen in the work of many educationalists (see McNiff, 2002). However, for others it remained at the level of problem-solving for teachers. They were not concerned to develop a new educational science nor did they take a critical stance on the basic values and actions in their practice. This second, rather narrow approach to teachers as researchers may be seen in the utilitarian approach taken by many politicians and managers. Thus in these two views of action research we can see reflected the differing perspectives on teacher professionalism discussed earlier.

Throughout the late 1980s and 1990s, when teachers were subject to increasing pressure and a rising number of directives from central government, many critics saw action research as too micro in scale and somewhat insular. Thus, as teachers appeared to be losing control over the curriculum, action research seemed increasingly irrelevant in the face of wider political pressures. The assumption that teachers had the power to change their practice rather than being constrained by wider pressures now appeared rather naive (Avis, 2001). The underpinning social democratic ideology being promoted in the curriculum developments of the 1960s, 1970s and even the early 1980s, was replaced by that of neoliberalism and competition. Certainly, the image of the extended profes-sional does not sit comfortably within an environment of increasing central control and the development of market forces that has taken place in education over the last 20 years.

■ ■ ■ School effectiveness and school improvement research

The adoption and development of managerialist strategies in the 1980s with their aim of increasing efficiency by improving results and reducing costs led to a growth of interest in what became known as school effec-tiveness research. As its title implies, this approach sought, by using quantitative analysis, to identify what led to the creation of effective schools. Perhaps the first significant study in Britain using this approach that caught the public imagination was *Fifteen Thousand Hours* by Rutter et al. (1979). Using statistical techniques comparisons of schools were made that identified the factors that set more successful schools apart from the less successful. Over the years lists of these characteristics have been added to and refined by a number of studies (see Creemers, 1994; Reynolds et al., 1994; Sammons et al., 1995; Teddlie and Reynolds, 2000). These lists tend to be very similar, usually citing strong and effective lead-ership, high expectations of pupil achievement and behaviour, an orderly atmosphere with an emphasis on learning, monitoring of pupil progress and clear enforced discipline with positive reinforcement of success.

However, various criticisms have been levelled at school effectiveness research (see Carter, 1998; Elliott, 1998; Thrupp, 2001; Willmott, 1999). The data collected was statistical and there were issues concerning the accuracy of its measurement. Indeed it was questionable as to whether an agreed definition could even be arrived at for many of the factors, such as 'an orderly atmosphere' or 'effective leadership'. The term 'effective' is itself a value-laden term when applied to education. There are different opinions as to what constitutes an effective school, or effective teaching. Many felt that this research considered effectiveness from a managerial perspective only. It became tied to measurable outcomes and these were then taken as important outcomes of education. Thus examination results and truancy figures may be used to judge effectiveness but not the happiness of pupils or the job satisfaction of the teachers. Many of the factors linked to effective schools by this research were not startling in themselves and were already regarded as important issues in schools. The difficulty for schools was to actually develop the traits that were seen as linked to effectiveness. So, whilst identifying and developing lists of what could be seen as almost common-sense factors linked to school effectiveness, this research gave no indication of how schools could work towards these. As this research was carried out by 'outside' researchers rather than teachers, the findings often appeared as another presentation of management ideology being passed down from above. The result was that they were often treated with cynicism by those working in schools.

The disillusionment with the positivist approach of school effectiveness research and its associated ideology was countered by the development of the 'school improvement movement'. This has the individual school at its centre and through a research approach seeks to develop and implement strategies that will lead to improvement. It encourages a more eclectic approach to data collection and can therefore take a less restricted view of what is meant by school improvement. School improvement research sees the school as a community and recognizes the importance of those with a 'stake' in the findings being involved in the research (see Hopkins, 2001; 2002; Hopkins and Harris, 2000). It is through the school improvement movement that the notion of teachers as researchers, developed under the action research movement, was maintained throughout the 1990s. It is interesting to note that there was a move towards a more eclectic approach, that encouraged the use of aspects of both the school effectiveness and the school improvement approaches to research on schooling (Carter, 1998). Others, however, held that effectiveness and improvement research are predicated on different ideologies of education that make any future merger of the two approaches impossible (Elliott, 1996; 1998; Halsall, 2001).

Whilst the notion of teachers as researchers seemed increasingly out of place in the Conservative administrations from 1979 until 1997, the climate changed somewhat under the 'New Labour' administration. Research continued to be focused on school improvement perspectives but talk of partnerships in education with all stakeholders working together to raise standards became the norm. There was also a re-examination of the professional nature of teaching. The Labour government appeared to recognize the importance of teachers developing their classroom skills and how this might be achieved through reflective practice. The promotion of teachers researching their own classroom practice was formally encouraged through DfEE funding of Best Practice Research Scholarships (DfEE, 2000b). However, the focus of this research has been firmly in the classroom and on raising (largely measurable) standards. Funding made available through both the TTA and the DfEE has tended not to encourage wider questioning of the purposes of education nor where these standards have come from. As such this research has done little to create communities of teacher researchers and has promoted largely restrictive professional development (Bottery and Wright, 1999). Such policy-driven outcomes have been referred to by Patrick et al. (2003: 239) as the dual ambiguity of autonomy–performativity. In other words, government is deploying the language of empowerment and professional autonomy whilst using funding to coerce a focus on measurement of performance. This narrow focus on classroom and pupil performance may explain why practitioner research and evidence-based practice is presented as a new initiative with the broader vision of many action researchers from the past not mentioned. We contend, however, that to some extent a Stenhousian approach will be revived as teachers gain more confidence in their new research skills and begin again to ask questions about the purposes and nature of learning. The introduction of government funded Networked Learning Communities (www.ncsl.org.uk/nlc), designed to promulgate and share best practice amongst schools, has created a context where teacher researchers can collaborate on their research. It will be interesting to see the effects of these communities in the development of broader approaches to researching practice. A joint National Foundation for Educational Research/General Teaching Council/British Educational Research Association (NFER/GTC/BERA) project on education for sustainable development recently emphasized the value of such collaborations in encouraging practitioners to go beyond research dissemination to research utilization (Rickinson et al., 2003).

■ ■ ■ What is practitioner research?

The field of practitioner research involves a wide variety of professional and community contexts such as health care, social work, police work and schooling. These contexts create differences in the approaches practitioners use but characteristic of each is 'a central commitment to the study of one's own professional practice by the researcher himself or herself, with a view to improving that practice for the benefit of others' (Dadds and Hart, 2001: 7). Thus practitioner research in education can be seen as any research carried out by teachers and other education professionals, such as teacher trainers, educational advisers, education social workers, into aspects of their work. This research can be carried out for a variety of reasons and can take many forms. The research may be conducted as part of a credit-bearing course at graduate or postgraduate level. Alternatively, the research could be an element within a curricular/performance evaluation involving a team of teachers. It may be classroom focused on an issue of particular interest or concern to a teacher; equally it could be considered to be in the interests of the whole school. Pursuing a small-scale piece of research may have been identified as a useful part of professional development for a teacher or group of teachers.

Many teachers, after having gained several years' practical classroom experience, wish to return to an academic study of education. For these teachers practitioner research is often a way of revisiting theory they have not studied since their student days. Thus practitioner research can be initiated for a number of reasons, from a desire to learn more about teaching and learning or to return to more formal academic study and gain higher qualifications, to the pursuit of practical solutions to the evaluation of practice. From this broad set of motives we can see that practitioner research needs to embrace a whole host of approaches. In contrast, government-funded initiatives have tended to focus explicitly on classroom practice concerned to gather 'hard' data on what works. McNamara and Rogers (2002) for instance, describe the TTA, which was sponsoring their research, as displaying a narrower conception of peda-gogic research than the researchers themselves. Thus teachers, whilst remaining classroom based, may also wish to consider teaching and learning in a wider context that acknowledges the contested and com-plex nature of the education process.

The reasons for embarking upon a practitioner research project will certainly have an effect upon the choice of area of investigation by the researcher. The divide between classroom-based research that has a prac-tical purpose and academic research that is theory driven is often overstated. There is a complex interweaving of theory and practice that cannot be ignored. Thus, theoreticians must base their research upon what actually happens for it to have any meaning, whilst those seeking practical solutions will also need to consider theoretical explanations for their results. As teachers become more involved in classroom research, they seek out the relevant associated literature and thus often become increasingly involved in 'theory'. Many beginning practitioner researchers start with a classroom focus and they come to increasingly confront broader educational issues as they progress. Other teachers begin with a wider education policy interest, perhaps fuelled by studying for a master's degree, and then focus down onto specific areas of their classroom for research-based assignments.

Invariably there are significant philosophical questions of purpose that lie behind our research and these can never be ignored. Thus, when researching into the developing of literacy and numeracy skills in pupils, questions arise as to the identification and measurement of these skills and also the worth we place upon them. This in turn is likely to lead to at least some reflection on the basic purposes of schooling and education. The research process helps to remind us of the sets of beliefs and values upon which education is based. Whilst the encouragement of teachers as practitioner researchers is to be welcomed, it is important that this encompasses a broad approach to education and its role in society. We should be continually striving towards an extended view of professional development if we are to progress beyond what can remain a very narrow approach to educational research. It is also important to recognize this research publicly so that it influences policy as well as practice – 'to close the circle' as Evans et al. (2000: 415) describe it.

■ ■ ■ Conclusion

We have seen how today's notion of the practitioner researcher has some resonance with the action research movement. In charting, from a historical perspective, the growth of different forms of teacher and school research, we have learned how significant government policies are in shaping and influencing these research approaches. In the next chapter we examine some examples of practitioner research that illustrate the way in which initial research approaches are often adapted as the researcher learns more about the issues they seek to understand.

■ ■ ■ Task: Comparing published educational research

Read a copy of both the *British Educational Research Journal* and the *Educational Action Research Journal* since the year 2000. Compare their approaches in terms of:

■ focus of the editorials
■ range of research methodologies
■ scope of articles.

■ ■ ■ Suggested further reading

British Educational Research Association (BERA) (2003b) *Issues and Principles in Educational Research for Teachers.* Southwell, Notts: BERA.

This booklet has been written for teachers interested in undertaking research. It raises key issues and offers general principles for good practice. It is well presented and accessible to those approaching educational research for the first time. It is a very useful starting point for any intending practitioner researcher.

McNiff, J. with Whitehead, J. (2002) *Action Research: Principles and Practice.* 2nd edn. London: RoutledgeFalmer.

This text discusses the principles and practices of action research. It provides a useful analysis of the theoretical underpinnings of action research and how they may be applied. Case studies are used to illustrate the part played by theory and reflection.

▪ ▪ ▪ Chapter 4

Best practice case studies: evolving research approaches[1]

▪ ▪ ▪ Introduction

The DFES-sponsored initiative of Best Practice Research Scholarship (BPRS) for teachers, which ran from 2000 to 2004, generated small-scale projects in schools across the country.

This chapter shows, through a number of BPRS case studies, that a positivist approach to research often does not help teachers to gain the understanding of their classrooms that they seek. Practitioners should be aware of, and not afraid to use, interpretivist approaches that are often more suitable to their needs.

▪ ▪ ▪ Background to the teachers' research

Best practice research scholarships were introduced from September 2000. They were funded by the DfEE to 'enable teachers to undertake classroom-based and sharply focused small scale studies in priority areas, and to apply and disseminate their findings' (DfEE, 2000b: 1).

It was expected that the teachers would use various research methods such as observation, interviews and questionnaires, and make use of existing relevant data and documents where appropriate. This was recognized as a useful way of building knowledge and understanding about raising standards of teaching and learning among those chosen as teacher researchers. It would also benefit their schools and other schools who could share the lessons learned. Thus dissemination and sharing of findings was seen to be very important, alongside the benefits gained by those teachers participating in the research process itself. Year-long scholarships would usually be between £2,500 and £3,000. This funding was to cover the costs of research, for example, some supply cover to enable the teacher researcher to collect data in lesson time. Much of the scholarship awarded was to pay for the support of the novice teacher researcher in the research process by experienced mentors. In this way it was expected that the teachers would develop the required research skills and be more likely to successfully complete the research project.

Three cases of teacher research are used to illustrate the importance of values, ideologies and perspectives that cannot be ignored when designing and carrying out research. They were taken from two clusters of teachers, seven in all, who were awarded best practice scholarships for the academic year of 2001/02. They all worked with the same mentor from a university college and they were organized into these two small clusters to encourage mutual support through the process. As mentor to these best practice researchers, Bartlett had also worked with a group of BPRS teachers the previous year. Although finding this generally a positive experience, certain reservations were noted in terms of time constraints and the expectations of the teachers on the effects of their research (see Bartlett, 2002). There was also some disquiet over an approach which was primarily about application of methodological tools with little consideration of underlying philosophies of research and knowledge.

As with the first group of best practice researchers, this second cohort followed a programme where, in several initial meetings over the autumn term, there was an emphasis on the tools of research, devising research questions and the planning of their research project. This process seemed to progress relatively smoothly and in the second term the focus changed to monitoring the research projects as they unfolded and to the sharing of experiences. It was expected that in the following autumn, all projects could be formally presented at a teacher researcher conference. In monitoring progress and sharing experiences in the second and third terms issues which had surfaced with the previous group of best practice researchers began to emerge again.

As the second term progressed the mentor wrote a reflective account of each of the best practice researchers' progress. These included a description of what each teacher had decided to do and of how their project had evolved. They were based on the group meetings, individual tutorials, phone conversations and e-mails. In the summer term when the teachers had resolved their issues in one way or another the teachers were given the written accounts to read. This was done for two reasons. The first was to ascertain if the teachers considered the perceptions of the mentor reasonable and the second was to see if they could recognize their development over the year from someone else's perspective. The response from the teachers was very positive – they did agree with the commentary, felt pleased that the accounts had been written and seemed genuinely interested to read them. These mentor accounts promoted discussion and enabled an airing of a research process that had made them feel insecure at many times in the year when they had to question their beliefs about data, the nature of research, what they 'should' be doing and how this was not quite the same as what they had set out to do. In many ways it helped them to focus more on what they had actually achieved and how their understanding of research had changed.

Within the cohort there are a wealth of examples of teacher research in different types of schools, examining a range of issues in varying circumstances. Some teachers are able to carry out their small-scale research with few problems. They are able to identify their research issue, gather data, analyse it and write a research report, all within the prescribed timescale. The majority of teacher researchers, however, had to grapple with a range of methodological issues during their research. These three cases have been chosen in particular because they clearly identify serious ideological and methodological problems which both teacher researchers and mentor had to face when accepting an instrumentalist view of best practice research. They illustrate factors that apply to large numbers of teacher researchers to varying degrees.

■ ■ ■ Teacher 1 Part-time special needs teacher in a primary school

This teacher was working with pupils with short attention spans who found it difficult to concentrate in lessons, were unable to complete work, produced little in the way of quantity and quality, and as a result were a disruptive influence in the classroom. More often than not they were kept in at break to complete work and this meant the added frustration of not getting out to play. The teacher researcher wanted to see the effect that working with computers had on these children. She suspected that working on computers held their concentration for longer and enabled them to produce more work. She found a programme on literacy and numeracy, which was similar in content to the work they are normally given. Using the computers for literacy and numeracy these pupils were now completing tasks and they were working in a more methodical manner.

The teacher did work alongside the pupils when they began working on the computer programme but this was part of their normal routine anyway. She then began to leave them more on their own and found that they were remaining on task. From time to time their attention did wander but they returned to carry on where they had left off. The teacher did wonder why they were paying more attention and if the effect would wear off in time. There is the novelty factor but these were not computer games and the tasks were repetitive. She suspected that the screen was able to grab their attention far more than working with paper and pencil does. When writing on paper they could lose concentration, make a mess or a mistake and were then stuck with it. This used to put them off going back to the task. Now the pupils did not have to suffer for their mistakes as these could be deleted. She noted that sometimes the pupils play with the mouse and keys for a long time but are still able to return to their work. Since using the computers, these pupils are producing more work and of a higher standard than previously. The teacher now wants to see if this progress is maintained.

The teacher researcher had carefully watched these pupils and noted how their behaviour had changed. She was able to clearly explain what had happened throughout the research. However, she was worried that she had no 'proper' data. Findings were based on her observations only. There were no formal measures of achievement. She did have their work but did not feel that this was valid research evidence.

When encouraged not to worry about lack of quantitative data she began to realize that her observations were important and that she had noted important developments. These made a research diary that could be developed over time. In the next stage of her research she was going to bring the pupils' perspective into the research through talking (interviewing) with them. Qualitative rather than quantitative data is appropriate in these situations and this teacher researcher has increasingly come to terms with the reality that complex situations such as these cannot be easily measured. The important point for the teacher researcher is to remain critical and to look for what is happening, constantly checking and revisiting findings, basing judgements on evidence rather than opinion. This is exactly what this teacher has been doing, but for a long time she had felt guilty that this could not be considered as proper research.

Through carefully observing these pupils over time in this way, the teacher has developed her understanding of the motivational effects of working with computers almost without realizing her growing expertise.

▪ ▪ ▪ Teacher 2 Deputy head of a primary school

This study began with what was clearly a positivist/technicist view of research. The teacher worked in a particularly challenging school and felt that use of the interactive whiteboard had made her teaching more effective, especially for those pupils who generally had more difficulty in concentrating. The education action zone, of which her school was a member, had promoted the introduction of whiteboards and she wanted in her research to identify their effectiveness and so develop pedagogy.

The difficulty for this teacher researcher lay in identifying exactly what made the whiteboard so effective and then moving on to measure this. She initially decided to give similar lessons to a group of pupils with and then without the whiteboard. An observer would note pupils' behaviour and work rate which could be compared. However, it was proving difficult to set up an observation schedule of effective learning and she was still unsure why the whiteboard was better. The researcher then considered analysing pupil work produced after a whiteboard lesson and work produced after a 'normal' lesson.

The teacher researcher was becoming more reflective as she grappled with the problems of research design. Whilst working through the daily challenges she faced in her school she began analysing her practice in more detail alongside other aspects of classroom interaction. The search for clarification of the research focus had caused her to reconsider all aspects of her work as a teacher at a fundamental level. She came to acknowledge what she already knew through her teaching experience – that the whiteboard was really part of her overall teaching strategy and could only be evaluated as such.

Inspired by a local education authority (LEA) course she returned to an interest in how pupils learn. She wished to explore theories of learning style and how these operated in the classroom situation. She decided to set up a series of lessons using teaching approaches that would correspond to different learning styles. The effect upon particular pupils could then be noted. Pupils would be actively involved and their opinions sought as part of the research. The process could be repeated to show if their preferences fitted their learning styles and if they were consistent. This would be a starting point for her own investigations into learning. This teacher is following her own broader professional interests and is moving from research being used purely for technicist teaching purposes to look more deeply at learning. She is now less concerned with absolute measurements and more with descriptive accounts of change over time. She is also beginning to involve the pupils more in the process.

Once again we see that a qualitative approach to research may lead to a more extended form of professionalism. It took the teacher time to come to terms with this approach, having been brought up with a belief that hard measures were what mattered and were required. In a fascinating juxtaposition of the 'hard' and 'soft' stories of the same research project, Walsh and Hustler (2002) concluded that although, in the 'hard version', their research might be construed as methodologically flawed, its worth in helping the teachers in the school to reassert their professionalism was undoubted. The teachers began regularly to discuss pedagogical strategies, to observe each other teaching and to ground their discussions in evidence.

■ ■ ■ Teacher 3 Deputy head of a primary school

This teacher originally wanted to look at effectiveness of different methods of teaching spelling using an experimental research design. It was hoped that several teachers could be involved and that they could either teach their classes differently and results could be compared or they could each use a different method for several weeks and then see the results from marks obtained from spelling tests.

The researcher first had to grapple with the fact that different methods of teaching spelling are not mutually exclusive and that teachers could not be expected to ignore other methods if appropriate to pupils in a particular instance. That left the researcher having to look at her own class and doing the research herself. She still had to face the ethical problem of sticking to one method of teaching spelling rigidly over a time. Feeling rather ensnared in issues of research design, and because of teaching pressure at school, she decided to leave the project until well into the spring term. Over the next few months thinking of how to carry out her research took this teacher back to a basic consideration of what teaching involved and how complex the process was. This in turn led her to question how children were learning in different ways. This was something she felt was important and more appropriate than the narrow approach she had been taking on methods of teaching spelling. This still left a problem of what she should research as the scholarship year was nearly halfway through. A decision was made in discussion with the mentor to investigate learning through current research literature and to look at her own classroom for examples of how pupils learned differently. This whole exercise would be useful professional development for the teacher and could be developed further in the future as appropriate.

The teacher was still concerned about what would constitute the research. It was decided to set up different teaching situations and to observe how the pupils responded, to look at their work and to ask them about how they found the different learning situations. Though learning style is a very complex area and the teacher is only beginning her research, she is taking the opportunity to learn more about the effects of her teaching and how her pupils learn. The research is in her own hands and is being done in her classroom at a rate within her control. It is involving pupils and getting responses from them. She is being proactive, asking questions, making observations and returning to academic literature for reference. Significantly, this reflexive approach allows the teacher researcher to consider and admit her own feelings and responses to the pupils' learning.

Again this is an example of where the teacher has moved from an overtly technicist approach to developing a broader perspective on the teaching and learning processes. The methods have become 'softer' to gain a deeper understanding of complex processes that do not lend themselves to quantitative measures. It could be argued that this is extended professional development and involves a more sophisticated awareness of the educative process by the teacher.

■ ■ ■ The significance of these cases

These teachers applied for the best practice scholarship grant as a result of an interest in their professional practice for a combination of reasons such as career advancement, personal interest in a particular aspect of teaching, a desire to become involved with higher education (HE) and perhaps participate in further study. Most had little or no experience of conducting educational research and little interaction with research literature. Hannan et al. (2000) found that, compared with medical practitioners, teachers were less involved or interested in professional research literature, reflecting perhaps its traditional lack of importance for career advancement.

Many of the teachers beginning BPRS had a preconceived view of research based upon a traditionalist scientific or positivist paradigm. Research was seen as being carried out on an experimental model in an objective manner, producing measurable, largely statistical data that was beyond dispute. Research set out to prove or disprove a particular point and the results could thus be clearly applied. The literature and application process for the BPRS grants encouraged this view, as did government emphasis on research which could clearly identify best practice and which all teachers should use in their professional development.

The teachers had not considered the research/evaluation skills which they already possessed and used on a daily basis in the classroom. They had a low opinion of the worth of their individual judgements as being valid for the purposes of curriculum development. It would appear that after years of working under prescribed guidelines, in terms of curriculum, assessment and inspection, they expected good practice to be a given which they aspired to. As in Ebbutt et al.'s study (2000), the teachers were also very aware of their 'audience', that is, the head and other teachers, and the imperative for the research to lead to perceived change within a short timescale.

The programme drawn up by the mentor provided a 'tool-box' approach to research. This was due to the limited time available and a pressure to 'get the research done'. However, it assumed an awareness in the teachers of the nature of research and data collection. It did not encourage reflection on the philosophies underpinning research. Thus it promoted a narrowing rather than expanding of the teachers' focus.

The difficulty of designing research, which could be carried out in a straightforward manner to yield concrete, clearly visible, comparable data and demonstrate cause and effect, called into question the initial assumptions of the teachers concerning research. In group sessions the complex nature of classroom life became an issue which, it was now realized, had tended to be overlooked when considering best practice. The teachers also began to question what they had originally set out to do and began to discuss fundamentals concerning the nature of teaching and learning. This initially raised anxieties in that they were unsure as to the legitimacy of discussing such topics. However, technical teaching issues, such as how to raise spelling scores, now appeared less fundamental and interesting than the wider debates surrounding teaching and learning. This was not to say that spelling scores were unimportant but that they needed to be placed into the context of the whole education of the pupil. As the year progressed, once the teachers felt comfortable with the notion of open forum and the realization that their views were interesting to other teachers in the group, discussion moved to all areas of education.

In order to be able to follow their interests the teachers needed a different, more reflexive, approach. They had to use the experience they had gained of informal interview with, and unstructured observation of, pupils to its full advantage. They had to view their classroom in a different way, anthropologically strangely, and to interpret what they found. From discussion over the year it was clear to the mentor that these teachers could interpret 'data' and that they were critical. However, they had relied on being told what was good teaching for so long that they felt insecure in setting their own research agenda and making judgements themselves without reference to the official view.

Growing awareness of the situated nature of research into classrooms made these teachers more comfortable with different forms of data collection and aware of the need to interpret the data themselves. Their fear of bias was to some extent counterbalanced by using various methods, different accounts and sharing results with respondents and other teachers. The aim was to be honest and rigorous in what they had done, to develop their own understanding of different aspects of education and, hopefully, for their accounts to be relatable to other teachers. Rather than worrying about whether or not their research was truly objective they needed to continually reflect upon whether they had presented their findings reasonably and fairly. They were becoming more comfortable with the part values play in the action research process (Bassey, 1998). This approach also allows teacher researchers to involve others, such as colleagues and pupils, in the research. It becomes a more collaborative experience altogether. Harris and Anthony (2001) describe how such collegial networks of teachers are a long-established form of in-service education in Japan and are now being adopted in North America,

Israel and the UK as a legitimate way of promoting teacher development.

Some of the teachers were now more interested in looking at what was actually happening in their classroom rather than being focused upon particular quantitative targets relating to pupil achievement that had been set externally. This resulted from asking basic questions such as 'How do children learn?' 'In what ways do they learn differently?' 'How do the different theories of learning style relate to my classroom?' Thus accounts of their research started to emerge that were relevant to other teachers. These promoted discussion and encouraged broader reflection of the education process. The issues were ones which the best practice teacher researchers themselves wanted to explore but had been made to feel were inappropriate. What appears to have happened in these three cases is that the narrow guidelines for research encouraged by the DfES in its drive to raise standards had rekindled a desire to develop the BPRS teachers' theoretical as well as practical understandings. Campbell (2002) similarly found that her teacher researchers developed confidence in their ability to discuss their practice, developing a language of professional discussion. And in the USA Kraft (2002: 188) concluded that research structured around principles of critical self-reflection assisted teachers 'in their teaching/learning transactions and how to more effectively mediate the curriculum to their students'.

Discussion and critical reflection seems to be leading to the development of a more extended professionalism. Whilst these cases have been specifically chosen as being good examples of this process, we wish to argue that this will apply to some extent to the majority of teachers who engage in practitioner research of this nature. In order to promote this extended professionalism, what is needed in future is an approach to research which emphasizes the complex nature of the classroom, the value of reflexivity and the importance of continuing to ask the 'big questions' about the purposes of education. Webb (2002) found that, in one US state, teacher researchers began to exercise some autonomy over mandated curricular and assessment policies as a consequence of their more sophisticated levels of thinking about teaching and learning. Their prior learning, professional development and practitioner enquiry had all contributed to their deepened understanding. Thus the inclusion of a reflexive approach as part of a continuous process of professional development is highly appropriate if we are to maximize teacher professionalism and, concomitantly, improve pupil learning.

■ ■ ■ Conclusion

Whilst a research approach that is practice based and concerned with improving standards using a positivist methodology may at first sight seem alluring, it proves difficult to reduce many important influences of classroom life to simplistic, easily measurable elements. This is realized by many teacher researchers who, being more aware of the complex nature of education, are turning to more qualitative approaches in their search for a deeper professional understanding. This will continue to be the case as the confidence to question more widely grows and teachers move away from the narrow approaches to education and research that have been promoted in the last decades of the twentieth century. This should help reinstate a place for teachers' voices in education policy-making arenas. The ensuing chapters take us into the detail of embarking upon a research project and employing a range of data collection strategies.

■ ■ ■ Task: Exploring practitioners' understandings of research processes

Interview two or three teachers who are currently involved in research. They may be working within a networked learning community, studying for a Masters or Doctorate degree or conducting a small-scale project identified within their school or professional development plan. Try to find out how they determined and developed their research approach, and whether their views of the research processes they employed have altered.

■ ■ ■ Suggested further reading

Dadds, M. and Hart, S. (2001) *Doing Practitioner Research Differently*. London: RoutledgeFalmer.

Through six case studies this book considers why practitioner researchers need to be adaptable and it puts the case for practitioner researchers to resist 'methodological dogma'. This volume encourages practitioner researchers to think creatively when designing their research.

McNamara, O. (ed.) (2002) *Becoming an Evidence-Based Practitioner: A framework for teacher researchers*. London: RoutledgeFalmer.

This is an edited collection of case studies of practitioner research. It illustrates teachers working in collaboration with LEAs and local universities to design and conduct classroom research projects. This book gives a flavour of real practitioner research to those readers about to take the plunge.

[1] Bartlett, S. and Burton, D. (2003) 'The professional development of teachers through practitioner research: a discussion using significant cases of best practice research scholarships', *Teacher Development*, 7(1): 107-19.

■ ■ ■ Chapter 5

Getting started: beginning a research project

■ ■ ■ Introduction

This chapter outlines the initial planning that is required if a research project is to be carried out successfully. Before embarking on the research process the researcher needs to have carefully thought through the purpose and precise focus of the research. These are key factors that will shape the whole project. They will determine the scale, detail and writing up of the final results.

■ ■ ■ Designing a research project

The researcher needs to turn their initial ideas into a research outline/strategy. This is usually termed a 'research proposal' when applying for grants, funding or admission to a research degree programme. There is a need to construct a structured plan that identifies what is going to be investigated, how the research will be carried out and what will be the expected outcomes in terms of data and analysis. This all needs to be put in a time frame, so a detailed time line needs to be written that gives targets to work towards. Experienced teachers are used to working in such time frames, which they have devised themselves or are externally imposed. In school development planning, for example, targets are set, specific tasks are carried out in order to achieve these, there is regular evaluation of progress and further reviewing all within a clearly defined time frame. Teachers, working in curriculum teams, design and implement schemes of work by largely the same process. This planning is also carried out by the individual teacher who through a school's performance management process is expected to set personal targets linked to professional development. These are reviewed as part of an annual cycle.

Whilst it is important to have a clear plan by which to operate, this must not be allowed to become too rigid. The researcher must be prepared to adapt and change according to altering circumstances. Many things may happen concerning the focus of the research or the circumstances of the researcher that can cause substantial alterations to the original plans. Sometimes the final research project is very different to that which was initially intended. However, it is useful to start with as clear a plan as possible. This will at least give a feeling of security for the researcher at the start of what can be perceived as a rather risky and threatening process. See Punch (1998) for a further discussion of developing research proposals.

Research is about asking questions (Clough and Nutbrown, 2002) and then gathering data to help answer these questions. However it can develop into an ever-expanding process if not managed effectively. It is possible to ask what seems like a never-ending stream of questions that become progressively wider in scope and leave one feeling very unclear about where the research should be going. What is needed initially is the development of a clear focus of investigation. Ideally, it should be possible to explain the focus in a paragraph which states what is to be researched and why. By having a focus, or main aim/purpose, it should then be possible to ask what it is we specifically want to find out concerning this focus, that is, what the particular issues are. This will highlight the important questions to which we need to find the answers, in other words, the key research questions.

Thought should simultaneously be given to a title for the research project. The title will become easier to write as the focus becomes clearer. A good title should signify clearly and concisely the topic of the research and the target group that make up the respondents. It should indicate the parameters of the research, for example, clarifying whether it is a case study of one example or involves large samples.

■ ■ ■ Research questions

The key research questions should be worked up at the same time as the focus and title. All three, focus, title and research questions, are part of the initial developments of the research proposal.

What are research questions? These are questions that require researchers to 'define the limits of their study, clarify their research study, identify empirical issues and work on empirical questions' (Clough and Nutbrown, 2002: 33). They identify precisely which aspects of the area of interest should be researched, they indicate sources from which information can/should be obtained and also appropriate ways of collecting this information (Lewis and Munn, 1997). We will now consider how research questions can be developed from a particular focus.

Pupil truancy: an example of designing research

In a secondary school staff became aware of an increasing truancy problem. This had always been an issue but the problem was raised in a staff meeting by one of the pastoral heads. Open discussion amongst staff indicated certain worrying trends that some teachers had noticed, such as an apparent increase in the number of pupils on the corridors during lesson time, instances of when some pupils had not been in lessons when teachers had seen them previously in the day. It was reported that local shopkeepers had rung the school concerning pupils in school uniform 'hanging around' the local shopping centre during school hours. Thus truancy of pupils during school hours became identified as an issue needing investigation, to be followed by effective action. An action group is formed and in its initial meeting a series of research questions are identified through a brainstorming session. Through discussion these are placed into major and sub-questions:

1. What is the current extent of pupil truancy?

   (a) How many pupils are truanting?

   (b) Which pupils are truanting? (Boys, girls, age, ability)?

   (c) When are these pupils truanting?

   (d) How frequently?

   (e) For how long do they truant?

2. Why are the pupils truanting?

(a) Is there an issue with particular lessons?

(b) What part does peer pressure play on truanting?

(c) Is truancy related to academic progress; if so, is it a result or cause of poor performance by truants?

(d) To what extent is truancy related to wider social issues outside school?

(e) Do their parents or other adults know of their truancy?

3. What do truants do?

(a) Where do they go?

(b) Are they usually alone or with friends also truanting?

(c) Are they involved in delinquent or criminal activity whilst truanting?

(d) Are they working for money whilst truanting?

4. What can be done to tackle the problem of truancy?

(a) What are the suggestions of staff, pupils, parents?

(b) What have other schools tried and how successful have they been?

(c) What suggestions have come from national and international research?

These can be seen as the first attempt at designing a set of research questions. They may change as the research progresses – they may be refined, added to, and so on. By formulating research questions the action group is beginning to put some structure around their focus and is now in a position to develop a plan to carry out the research. In this particular case four main questions have been asked with sub-questions within them. It is clear from this that four distinct things need to be found out: Q1. What is the extent of the problem? This involves the sub-questions of who, when, how often. When there is a clearer idea of what is happening and who is taking part it becomes possible to find out why these pupils are truanting (Q2). This can only be done when the true extent of the problem is known as many truants will be missed in the research if data is only gathered from particularly high-profile pupils, who are known truants to the staff. Linked to the question of why pupils truant is the issue of what they do whilst truanting (Q3). On the basis of data gathered from the first three questions what can be done to tackle the problem can then be explored (Q4).

The research questions have provided a clear trail to follow. It is now possible to identify what data needs to be gathered and who it should be collected from. That leads to the next step which is designing the appropriate methods by which to gather this data (Figure 5.1). There is thus a progression from developing research questions, to identifying data needed to answer these questions, to designing appropriate methods that can be used to gather this data.

Research questions	Sources	Methods
1 What is the extent of truancy in school X?	Staff, pupils	Attendance checks, cameras, corridor sweeps, pupil interviews, staff interviews

(a) How many pupils are truanting?
  (b) Which pupils are truanting? – boys, girls, age, ability
  (c) When are these pupils truanting?
  (d) How frequently?
  (e) For how long do they truant?		

2. Why are the pupils truanting?	Staff, pupils	Interviews/questionnaire
3. What do truants do?	Pupils	Interviews
4. What can be done to tackle the problem of truancy?	Staff, pupils, parents	Interviews/questionnaire

■ **Figure 5.1**

Data collection plan for truancy research

Though respondents and data collection instruments have been identified, important decisions still have to be made. Whilst it is possible to say that responses will be gathered from pupils and teachers, it still needs to be decided which pupils and teachers will be included in the research sample. It may also be difficult to obtain data from pupils on such a sensitive issue. Here the data collection methods decided upon and the skills of the researcher become important to the outcomes of the research. It is also easy to identify interviews and questionnaires as the main methods to be used but actually designing them can prove more difficult. As this is a first draft of the plan it is likely that there will be a number of changes as the teacher researchers learn more about truancy and are able to reflect upon their research as it develops. They may decide that some of the methods listed need to be carefully adapted to be more sensitive to the respondents. Other sources of useful data may also come to mind, for example, the experiences and opinions of parents, social services, youth workers, the police and the local shopkeepers who initially reported the issue may be sought.

Once the research questions have been developed it becomes possible to draw up a clear plan that the researchers can work with and which can be refined and developed over time. They need to consider practical research issues, the answers to which are linked to the intended size of the project such as the time and skills needed to design the various research methods, the collection and analysis of the data, and the presentation of findings. These form the content of the following chapters. Alongside this practical planning of the research process within the school, the action group will be aware of the need to draw on wider experiences. Other schools are likely to have tackled the problem of truancy and it would help to know if they carried out their own research and, if so, how they did it and what they found. It would also help to know what national and even international research has been done, what conclusions had been drawn, what strategies had been tried and how successful these had been. Thus there is a need to carry out a literature search to inform the research project being developed. With any piece of research a literature review forms a valuable section. Literature informs the compiling of research questions and research questions help, in turn, to identify areas of literature that need to be reviewed. The process of literature searches will be dealt with in Chapter 6.

There is the potential for a continuing spiral of practitioner research to be created from an initial investigation such as this. Various strategies for reducing truancy are likely to be suggested in answer to research question 4. The next stage would be to implement these with the teachers themselves evaluating their effectiveness through further research.

Having considered the designing of a research project we can identify some general guidelines on the forming of research questions. Research questions result from a brainstorming process, similar to that undertaken in the initial stages of curriculum design. Useful prompts which help in the framing of research questions include:

- Why research this area?

- What precisely is it that we want to find out about?

- Is there a desire to change anything? If so what and why?

- What/who are the likely sources of information and data?

- What are the views of colleagues on this research focus and what are their initial reactions to the study?

- What are the issues identified in the literature?

- What are the key findings of research already done?

■ ■ ■ Research time line

With the title written, the research focus clear, research questions in place and a literature search under way, it is now possible to construct a time line for the project. This will identify an order in which things can be done and give a realistic time by which to do them. A clear plan helps to ensure that nothing important has been missed out. It gives the researcher a programme to work through and a realistic completion date. This should enable the researcher to feel more in control of the process and able to manage the stress of deadlines. It should also allow the researcher to fit the research into existing work commitments. A plan, providing it is continually reviewed, actually enables the researcher to be more flexible and to adapt to unforeseen circumstances more effectively.

An example of a research time line

Jacky Bennison, a secondary school teacher with responsibility for pupil transition from KS2 to KS3, wanted to investigate to what extent her targeted activities in mathematics, with pupils near the end of Year 6 in their primary schools and early in Year 7 at the secondary school, made the move from primary to secondary school easier for these pupils. The research was to be carried out in the academic year 2002/03. She had already carried out targeted activities with Year 6 children in the feeder primaries in the academic year 2001/02 and was due to conduct more whilst they were now in Year 7 at her school. She intended to study a small sample group of these children in an attempt to evaluate the effect of these targeted activities on their transition from KS2 to KS3, with particular reference to their work in mathematics. Jacky had been awarded a best practice research scholarship. She designed the time line in Figure 5.2 under the questions posed as part of the best practice research grant application.

Questions from the BPRS application form:

■ How are you going to organize your time during the research?

■ What is your time line for identifying data?

■ When will you collect, analyse and interpret it?

■ How much time do you need to allow for writing up what you have done?

Time	Activity	People involved	Time	Cost
Preparation	Obtain permission from adults involved in project and from pupils' parents	All	1 wk	Photocopying costs
	Collate log of activities that had been carried out with primary school 2001–02	Researcher	1 wk	None
	Compile questionnaire about attitudes of pupils to the transition and to study of mathematics at Key Stage 3	Researcher and pupils	2 wks	Photocopying costs
Term 1	Firm research questions and undertake a literature search for relevant material	Mentor and researcher	3 wks	Mentor costs and library costs
	Further refine research methodology	Mentor and researcher	2 wks	Mentor costs
	Conduct initial interviews with small sample group	Researcher and pupils	2 wks	1 half day off timetable supply costs
	Conduct interviews with primary and secondary colleagues and LEA advisers to identify perceived problems of transition	Researcher, primary colleagues, secondary colleagues, LEA advisers	3 wks	2 half days off timetable supply costs

Term 2	Second interviews with sample group of pupils	Researcher and pupils	2 wks	
	Collaboration with members of the best practice group to analyse findings so far	Best practice group and researcher	3 wks	Mentor costs
	Questionnaire to whole of current group of Year 7 including small sample group to collect appropriate attitudinal data to check against findings so far	Researcher and pupils	2 wks	Photocopying costs
	Questionnaire to other teachers within mathematics department on small sample group's effort and attainment	Researcher and colleagues	2 wks	
Term 3	Check findings by conducting further taped interviews with two members of target group	Researcher and pupils	1 wk	1 half day off timetable supply costs
	Collaboration with colleagues at senior and primary level to aid interpretation of results	Researcher and colleagues	2 wks	1 half day off timetable supply costs
	Links made with reading and research undertaken by others	Best practice group, mentor and researcher	2 wks	Mentor costs
	Writing up of report	Researcher	3 wks	Photocopying costs
	Presentation of findings to staff at in-service training (INSET) with primary and LEA staff invited and presentation at university college	Researcher, senior and primary colleagues, LEA advisers BPRS group, mentor	2 wks	Mentor costs
	Submission of report to professional body	Researcher	1 wk	Photocopying and e-mail costs
	Submission of report to BPRS website and teacher development practitioner research unit at University College	Researcher	1 wk	e-mail costs

■ **Figure 5.2**

Research time line for a best practice research scholarship

The time line, when added to the research questions, gave the teacher a clear structure at the outset of her research. However she remained adaptable and did alter the time line as events developed.

Research projects can vary greatly. The design chosen will reflect the researcher's ideology of education and research, as noted in the previous chapters. It will also be influenced by the nature of the research focus, the respondents, and the resources available to the researcher.

■ ■ ■ Curriculum evaluations

Teachers often wish to use research methodology to monitor and evaluate a specific project they are implementing. In such cases it is even more important that the planning and time line are done before the commencement of the project. Figure 5.3 shows an initial planning pro forma used by a group of teachers introducing and developing curriculum projects as part of a networked learning community.

School ....
E-mail ....

Evaluation focus
In a few sentences outline your aims

List what will be done as part of the curriculum project
Think of structural changes, spending needed, teaching materials developed, pedagogic implications, in-service needs, specific events, pupil visits and so on

Outcomes
What do you hope will be achieved?

(Think of pupils, staff, others, any measures/indicators. Include important outcomes which may not be easy to measure)

How will we know?
What methods can be used for seeing/measuring what has been done/the process?
Identify how outcomes can be measured/identified. Who will be the respondents?
(Think of a broad range of methods)

(Later each method of data collection and a time line can be designed in detail)

■ **Figure 5.3**

Evaluation planning pro forma

The pro forma in Figure 5.3 was used by teachers in the North-West Learning Through Drama Network at the beginning of a two-year curriculum project funded by the DfES as part of the Developing Networked Learning Communities initiative. The group consisted of drama teachers from six secondary schools from north-west England. The schools that these teachers taught in varied enormously in size and in the social and ethnic mix of their pupil populations. The one thing that they had in common was that they were all specialist performing arts schools and therefore committed to the promotion of drama within their curricula.

Within the common theme of learning through drama, the teachers involved each identified a curriculum development that they intended to implement during the ensuing two years. They were going to evaluate these developments so that all the schools in the group could share the findings and then take them even further; it was intended that they could learn from each other. These were experienced teachers but they were unsure of their research skills. The issue for them was not so much the teaching involved in these innovatory projects but how they could carry out the evaluation in a way that was both accurate and useful. Thus a clear plan needed to be developed.

Using the planning pro forma

1. *Evaluation focus.* This section is to outline the curriculum development to be evaluated. It is effectively a statement and discussion of aims. These, when linked to the outcomes hoped for, effectively become the research questions of the evaluation.

2. *What will be done in the curriculum project?* Here the changes that need to/will be put in place to enable the development to take place are listed, for example, allocation of teaching hours, rooming and equipment requirements that need to be met, special training requirements of teachers/assistants. It will also outline the process that needs to take place such as changes in curriculum content, adaptation of teaching methods, and any special activities that need to be introduced. An example here could be the suspension of the normal timetable to allow pupils to work with a professional dance troupe.

3. *Outcomes.* This is a list or discussion of what it is hoped the out-

comes of the project will be. This is a clearer statement of how we judge if the aims have been met.

4. *How will we know?* Here the researchers identify from whom data will be collected and the methods that will be used to gather it. In these last two sections the evaluation team will need to consider the significance of different types of data, quantitative and/or qualitative, to their results.

The discussion by the evaluation/research team members that is required to fill out the pro forma serves to clarify what will be done in the curriculum development, how it will be done and the data that will show how successful this has been. It also allows us to move on to develop a time line showing when things will happen and when data will be gathered. This, in turn, will enable the identification of who will gather the data and analyse them. There is now a clear plan for the curriculum development and its evaluation and the teacher researchers are likely to feel more in control of the process. Each curriculum development presents unique problems as it unfolds. However, having devised a clear plan at the outset should help the practitioners cope with changing circumstances.

■ ■ ■ Networking for practitioner researchers

We have seen in earlier discussions of teacher professionalism and action research that the development of professionals involves learning from the work of others and reflecting upon their own practice. The whole notion of professional learning involves collaboration. Many researchers have noted the need to establish professional learning communities (Dadds and Hart, 2001; Walsh and Hustler, 2002). Working with peers and disseminating findings are thus important elements in practitioner research.

When carrying out research as part of an accredited programme, such as for a first degree, Masters, EdD or PhD, there is usually support for the practitioner researcher in the form of a research methods programme and the allocation of a dissertation tutor who will monitor progress and offer advice. However, when it comes to carrying out their own research, these students often still feel very lonely and isolated as each embarks upon their own personal project. A feeling of insecurity can be engendered by the research process when the researcher is conducting an individual and unique enquiry. In order to overcome this isolation, universities and colleges frequently arrange research students into groups that meet regularly to share ideas and experiences, and for the students themselves to give seminars on their findings. This can go some way to helping the researchers feel part of a group from whom they can draw support.

Many teachers begin as researchers by being part of an evaluation team of a curriculum development in their school. This often means that from the outset they are working with a group of colleagues. In this way they plan together, share ideas and discuss every stage of the process. This is an important phase in the development of the research project itself and of the research skills of the teachers. The research process is here clearly part of personal professional development. This networking is an important aspect of practitioner research (Bartlett, 2002).

■ ■ ■ Conclusion

In considering how to design and embark upon a research project, we have emphasized the importance of developing a clear focus and research questions. It is also important to be organized in terms of scheduling each stage of the research into a teacher's professional life. Finally, we have flagged up the value of collaborating with others in pursuit of the research enterprise. In Chapter 6 we discuss the significance of published research and other relevant literature to new research projects and consider how it can best be accessed and used.

■ ■ ■ Task: Planning a research project

The following activities will form the initial, planning stages of your research project. This plan will be further developed through the tasks at the end of subsequent chapters.

1. Using the appropriate sections of this chapter to guide you,

    (a) Identify a research focus.

> (b) Construct appropriate research questions.
> (c) Write a title for the project.
> 2. If you belong to a research group, place this initial plan on an OHT and present it to the group for discussion. This will enable you to refine the project in the light of supportive criticism.

■ ■ ■ Suggested further reading

Bell, J. (1999) *Doing Your Research Project: A Guide for First-Time Researchers in Education and Social Science.* Buckingham: Open University Press.

This is a set text for undergraduate students studying research methods. It is written for the novice researcher and takes the reader through the whole process from approaching a research issue to writing the final report.

Lewis, I. and Munn, P. (1997) *So You Want to Do Research! A Guide for Beginners on How to Formulate Research Questions.* Edinburgh: SCRE.

This is one in a series of short practical research guides published by the Scottish Council for Research in Education (SCRE). It is, as the title suggests, a guide on the writing of research questions for those new to research.

■ ■ ■ Chapter 6

Accessing and using literature

As researchers get deeper into their project the significance of existing research and relevant literature becomes clear. This chapter discusses the purposes of literature review, how and where to find relevant research or related literature and how to write it up within a study.

■ ■ ■ Purposes of literature review

Researchers need to access and review existing research and relevant literature in order to:

- provide background information on the general area of study

- describe and evaluate the context of the research (social, political, economic, educational, environmental, and so on)

- consider and comment on what has already been written within the general area of investigation, looking particularly at the relationships (differences and similarities) between studies

- discuss the relevance of existing research to the research focus and methodology (including any impact on the intended research questions).

To illustrate these four points, consider the following extracts from a paper the authors wrote on some small-scale research into the performance management of teachers:

[Background information]
Teacher education is increasingly conceptualized within an extended framework from initial training, through induction to the NQT year and beyond into qualified teacher status (Heaney, 2001). All teach-

ers are now subject to annual performance review. Performance management is seen as an ongoing cycle involving planning, monitoring and review (DfEE, 2000c) (Burton and Bartlett, 2002: 9).

[Describing the context]
The changes also include a 'fast track' through the profession to early subject leadership, senior management roles and on to headship (DfEE, 1999). Top quality graduates and 'the most talented serving teachers' will be selected for their commitment to teaching, excellent subject knowledge, and their talent to communicate, inspire and lead ... They will move more quickly through the pay scales and take up senior leadership roles within a few years of joining the teaching profession ... The creation of AST and fast track posts has been highly controversial as the availability of a few highly paid posts militates against a collegial approach to school improvement ... Thus the government's policy encourages a restricted view of professional activity with a narrow emphasis on the classroom and the techniques of teaching (Bottery and Wright, 1999). It also serves to fragment and divide groups of teachers who will be differentiated by their 'labels' and their salaries whilst the nature of their professional tasks will be fundamentally the same (Burton and Bartlett, 2002: 10).

[Commenting on literature on the general area of the research]
The performance management model also promotes a focus on the individual teacher as opposed to the subject or year team yet we know that much of the creative pedagogic and curriculum development work emanates from a team approach. This focus on individual development, and management by objectives, contrasts with a 'total quality management' model of development which emphasizes collaboration and teamwork (Deming, 1986, Scholtes, 1998). (Burton and Bartlett, 2002: 14).

[Relevance of existing research to research questions]
The linking of individual performance to pay may, rather than increasing the motivation of teachers, have the opposite effect, as suggested by the results of a Mori poll conducted after the first round of applications by teachers to cross the performance threshold (Mansell, 2001). Thompson (2000) suggests that teachers are not enthusiastic about individual pay initiatives. Thus a small-scale

impact study in which seven teachers from five schools in the north west were interviewed about their perceptions of, and attitudes towards, the performance management processes and threshold assessment payments in their schools, was conducted to address the following research questions:

How has performance management affected teaching effectiveness and pupil achievement?

How has achieving threshold status affected teachers as teaching professionals? (Burton and Bartlett, 2002: 15)

■ ■ ■ Types of available source material

The extent to which practitioner researchers can access a wide range of sources in conducting research projects will depend on how much writing and research they are used to doing and how much time they have available. Generally speaking, if one is looking for the latest research on a particular topic, journal articles are by far the best resource as they publish the most recent findings on highly specific issues. Many journals are published online making them even easier to access. Books tend to be longer in production and therefore any research referred to tends not to be so current. Books are usually better, however, for providing background information or policy overviews. Official publications such as government papers, for example from DfES, TTA and OFSTED, contain policy and strategy statements which are often essential for the researcher to understand the genesis of and motives for certain developments. Documents produced within schools and LEAs help provide factual and descriptive information to contextualize the research setting; they may also raise issues in relation to the research questions.

In education the pace of change is fast and developments can sometimes be dramatic so we require up to date commentary on new policy initiatives and the responses to them from teacher unions. Reputable newspapers such as the *Times Educational Supplement, Education Guardian* and *Independent Education* provide a useful service in this regard, often sourcing their pieces from educational experts. They provide information about developments in particular schools and publish the results from major research studies such as the Trends in International Mathematics and Science Study (TIMSS) which has compared the mathematics and science achievement of pupils across the world in 1995, 1999 and 2003. They also cover in detail the latest political and professional debates; of course, it is important to remember that all newspapers have licence for editorial bias! For certain information then, newspapers are a credible source to cite as long as they form only a small part of the material accessed.

▨ ▨ ▨ Writing literature reviews

If researchers are going on to present their work for an award-bearing course or to publish it in a journal or book, the whole study will need to be written up in a structured way. Many texts in our reference lists provide guidance on doing this. What follows here is some specific advice on writing literature reviews.

A literature review should convey an overview of the knowledge and ideas that have already been established on a topic and what their strengths and weaknesses are (Taylor and Proctor, 2001). Its guiding concept will be the research objective of the study for which the review has been undertaken. It should identify areas of controversy in the literature and formulate questions that need further research. It is also important to provide as balanced a view of competing perspectives as possible within the limits of the researcher's inevitable proclivity for a particular stance. The Evidence for Policy and Practice Information and Co-ordinating Centre (EPPI-Centre, 2003) produces 'systematic reviews' which aim to find as much as possible of the research relevant to particular research questions, and use explicit methods to identify what can reliably be said on the basis of these studies. Such reviews then go on to synthesize research findings in an easily accessible form which reduces the bias inherent in less rigorous approaches to review. Whilst researchers may find the outputs from these systematic reviews helpful the approach is not one they could emulate, since the process is very labour intensive and time consuming. It is neither possible nor desirable to review everything; the aim is to find studies of most relevance to the intended project and to isolate within each study the methodology and findings together with any underlying concepts, arguments or theories. The researcher then considers the implications of and relationships between these findings and suggestions in the context of their own focus of investigation. If writing up the project for a dissertation or article, the researcher will refer back to significant literature within their discussion of research findings in order to highlight any relationships between the new and the existing research.

It may be helpful initially in writing up a literature review to use a key overview text to describe the general area of study or 'map the terrain'. This can then be supplemented by drawing on related books, chapters, journals articles or news cuttings to develop the main structure of the argument and to support, add to or put a different slant on particular points. The basic approach is to start with the general and become ever more specific and precise as we home in on the research focus. It is always best to access the most up to date sources available as these should refer to any seminal work from the past as well as dealing with the latest research or policy developments.

Knowing when to use direct quotes from the literature is a skill that can be developed by reading existing reviews and papers. Generally, it is best to keep direct quotes to a minimum, attempting instead to weave an author's point into your own argument or indicating support for a point you are making by adding the author's name and date of relevant publication in brackets after the point. Direct quotes should only be used when, for maximum impact, the meaning needs to be unadulterated. The author's name, date of publication and page number of the quote should always be cited in the text, with the relevant reference included in the bibliography or reference list. The quote will need to be commented upon in order to justify its use and to retain the flow of the argument.

Sometimes it is easy to be drawn deeper and deeper into reading and fail to get down to any writing so the researcher needs to be disciplined enough to take frequent notes that summarize at intervals what the literature is saying in relation to the proposed new research. Reviewing literature is best done by writing in the researcher's own words, organizing notes around embryonic key arguments or points of enquiry. As the piece develops, structure will be critically important – the use of key headings each with their own subheadings or arguments helps to draw out the relationships between issues and findings systematically. The example below shows how this structure might work.

There is a great deal of interest currently in learning styles and many teachers embark on research studies in this field. The following example is an outline plan of what might be included in a fairly extensive review of learning styles research and literature.

Example: Outline plan for reviewing learning styles literature

- Introduction – Learning styles literature is extensive, varied and based on several different research approaches 'We will look at four distinct approaches and their respective research findings/researchers' positions' ...
- Key heading 1 – Learning styles
  Subheadings: Definition of learning style construct; Imager/verbalizer; Holist/serialist; Field-dependent/Field-independent; Visual/auditory/kinaesthetic; Relationships between categorizations; Implications for classroom
- Key heading 2 – Learning strategies
  Subheadings: Definition of learning strategy construct; Experiential learning – its characteristics; Kolb's cycle; Application to learners
- Key heading 3 – Learning approaches
  Subheadings: Definition of learning approaches construct; Motives for learning; Deep/surface learning; Approaches nurtured within UK classrooms/lectures
- Key heading 4 – Learning preferences
  Subheadings: Definition of learning preferences construct; Attitudinal and physical preferences; Learning preferences inventory; Relevance to different ages and stages of learners
- Conclusion – Summarize key features of the four different approaches; suggest the relative relevance of each to the context of the research; discuss potential application of one approach to the research project, indicating research questions it implies.

■ ■ ■ Conducting a library search

The following guidance is adapted from publications by Jackie Fealey and colleagues of the Liverpool John Moores University learning resource centre. It is applicable to most other library contexts.

A literature search is a systematic search through the many resources out-lined below in order to locate information on a given subject. It is essential to define a topic as closely as possible and consider any limits that could be applied, such as date or language of publication. Compil-ing a list of search terms, that is, keywords and phrases, which describe the subject is a good starting point. Using both British and American spellings where appropriate will ensure comprehensive coverage and including narrow and broad terms will enable the search to be narrowed if too much information is found, or to broaden it if the converse is true.

Books

Books in most libraries are arranged according to the Dewey Decimal Classification system. Within this system the subject of Education is clas-sified between the numbers 370–379, although the teaching of a subject above primary level is classified with the subject, for example, teaching primary mathematics is classed at 372.7 (with education), while teaching secondary mathematics is classed at 510.7 (with mathematics). As well as checking the stock on the shelves, researchers can usually search the library catalogue electronically in a number of ways including author, title, keyword and subject.

Journals

An increasing number of journals are now available electronically across the World Wide Web and the titles held in university libraries are listed in their catalogues; lists of the titles held electronically are easily avail-able from any good academic library and, if the institution pays a subscription fee to the publishers, researchers can gain access to full text electronic journals. Common search databases include:

■ Academic Search Elite: this multidisciplinary database offers full text for more than 1,850 scholarly journals, including nearly 1,300 peer-reviewed titles. Covering virtually every area of academic study, Academic Search Elite offers full text information dating as far back as 1985.

- Catchword: a database of online journals from leading academic publishers searchable by subject, publisher and by individual journal title.

- IngentaJournals: this provides online access to a selection of electronic journals published by leading scholarly publishers such as Blackwell Scientific and Academic Press. To access this service you require an Athens username and password.

- ScienceDirect: provides online access to over 1,000 Elsevier journals. It is possible to view abstracts or full-text articles including any photographs, tables or graphics featured in the printed article. The service also provides access to articles from 200 journals published by Academic Press (formerly known as IDEAL) and some other publishers.

Once connected to an electronic journal service, a known article can be selected or all the journals available through that service can be searched by subject or author's name.

Indexing and abstracting services

Indexing and abstracting services (often known as simply abstracts and indexes) are used to locate journal articles on particular subjects or by particular authors. They are published regularly (usually weekly, monthly or quarterly) and provide a means of keeping track of the thousands of journal articles that appear each year. The layout of each publication varies, but each service will provide sufficient information to enable researchers to locate the article in a library. Journals cited should be checked against the catalogue to see if they are held in the library or online. The following online service provides references to journal articles in Education.

- BIDS Education Service (www.dialogatsite.com) comprising British Education Index and ERIC, the American Education Index.

- Web of Science (http://wos.mimas.ac.uk/) contains three indexes: Science Citation Index (covering over 5,000 major scientific journals), the Social Sciences Citation Index (covering 1,700 core social science journals) and the Arts and Humanities Citation index (covering over 1,000 arts and humanities journals) from 1981 to date.

Athens personal passwords are required for these services – these passwords are available from libraries researchers are subscribed to.

Dissertations (theses)

Most academic libraries have collections of students' dissertations produced as part of higher degree courses such as MSc, MPhil or PhD. These can usually be referred to within the library but cannot be taken away or copied.

Dissertations are indexed in:

- British National Bibliography for report literature (1998–present)

- Index to Theses (ASLIB): an electronic version is available via the Electronic Journals and Datasets page.

Reports

Reports are issued mostly by research establishments, the government or private industry and are usually practical, up to date and detailed. Libraries have a selection of reports. Education reports are classified according to the subject of the report.

Newspapers

Newspapers can be very useful sources of contemporary reports and comment on new legislation and events. Libraries take a number of newspapers including daily broadsheets and the weekly education newspapers, the *Times Educational Supplement* and the *Times Higher Education Supplement*, back copies of which are available on microfilm usually from about the mid-1970s to the mid-1990s and thereafter on CD-ROM. Alternatively there are electronic newspapers' direct links available:

- Newsline (http://newsline.dialog.com/) provides to over 6,500 newspapers and magazines via the World Wide Web.

■ Daily Newspaper (http://dailynewspaper.co.uk/) provides access to all UK daily newspapers and thousands of links to newspapers worldwide.

The World Wide Web

The volume of information available via the Internet is expanding daily and provides an additional, if sometimes overwhelming, resource. It is best to search via a university library information page as this will have links to relevant sites such as the DfES, OFSTED and so on, electronic journals, special education sites, research bodies, publishers and lots of sites to support different curriculum subjects. However, researchers can strike out on their own by choosing one of the many search engines available and doing a keyword search of the whole. Caution is urged here as large amounts of information, often of dubious quality, will undoubtedly deluge the novice searcher.

Recording references

As the search progresses it is worth keeping details of potentially useful items encountered. If done accurately and consistently, useful material can be referred back to as the research develops. It also makes compiling the reference list, which should always appear at the end of the study, easy. A reference should always include the following basic information: who wrote the item, its year of publication, its title and who published it. It may be useful to include the place of publication. There are several ways of presenting this information. We recommend that you adopt the Harvard style and record references to books as follows:

Bell, J. (1999) *Doing Your Research Project: A Guide for First-Time Researchers in Education and Social Science*. Buckingham: Open University Press.

and references to journal articles as follows:

Aldrich, F. and Sheppard, L. (2000) '"Graphicacy": the fourth "R"?' in *Primary Science Review*, 64: 8–11.

■ ■ ■ Conclusion

We have seen how accessing previous research studies and relevant literature is essential to the development and refinement of a research project. Reviewing significant findings of other researchers not only helps to establish a sound platform for further research questions within a project but also plays a part in extending the body of research in the area. In this way, researchers of education act as a community to share and improve their understanding of a wide range of issues. In reviewing and commenting upon government reports or official policy documents practitioner researchers are able to outline and evaluate the policy issues germane to their research. Such literature, along with school and curriculum documentation, all contribute to the communication of a context for the project. Engaging with the literature is a fundamental part of the process by which researchers construct, review and reconstruct their views and questions about particular professional practices and their wider implications.

In Chapter 7 we turn to a consideration of case studies and experiments as strategies that teacher researchers may employ in their studies.

■ ■ ■ Task: Beginning a literature search

Use the focus decided upon when completing the task for Chapter 5 to begin a literature search; list a number of literature sources that:

- provide background information on the general area of study

- describe and evaluate the context of the research

- consider and comment on what has already been written within the general area of investigation

- discuss existing research relevant to the research focus and methodology.

■ ■ ■ Suggested further reading

Hart, C. (2001) *Doing a Literature Search*. London: Sage.

This is a comprehensive guide to planning and conducting a literature search. It explains how to find appropriate books, articles, official publications and statistics on a chosen research focus.

Woods, P. (1999) *Successful Writing for Qualitative Researchers*. London: Routledge.

This book considers all aspects of the writing up process. Even if they are not aiming for wider publication, all teacher researchers will be interested in the sections on organizing work, style and format, editing and collaborative writing. This is a useful text to read before commencing the final writing up.

■ ■ ■ Chapter 7

Research strategies: case studies and experiments

■ ■ ■ Introduction

This chapter outlines the case study approach, which is a very popular strategy with practitioner researchers. It also considers the use of experiments which, though in their purest form are only possible in highly controlled conditions, may be adapted to meet the needs of practitioner research.

■ ■ ■ Case studies

The case study approach is not a methodology as such but a research strategy where the researcher aims to study one case in depth. Work in the legal and medical professions is very much based upon case studies (see Hammersley and Gomm, 2000, for a discussion of the use of cases in varying contexts). Here particular cases are examined, usually in order to produce a solution or cure to the issue in question. Each case is unique, which is what makes them so interesting, however, the professionals involved are able to draw upon their knowledge of previous similar cases in order to understand the one currently being examined and to help them decide upon an appropriate ruling or action. For instance, since the law recently allowed parents to be prosecuted for truancy, the first test case which resulted in a mother being imprisoned has provided case law for similar prosecutions to be tested against.

Thus practitioners, in these fields that are looking at case studies, draw upon their own previous experience and documented accounts of previous cases to help them to analyse, explain and, where appropriate, suggest action. Their own findings can, in turn, be added to a growing body of case histories. This is a popular strategy in education research where using a case study approach enables teachers to research important aspects of their own working environment without being forced to collect large representative samples from a national frame. What actually constitutes a case is defined by the researcher and can vary enormously in size. Thus the case could be an LEA, a school, a class or a particular pupil.

By concentrating on a particular case or cases, data is usually collected by using several methods. Thus teachers are researching into classrooms and schools that they have existing knowledge of. Teachers are often able to use their own knowledge as a starting point and a descriptive account often sets the scene. They may then observe in a more detached way treating the case as anthropologically strange. Other data are typically collected from documents, records, photographs and interviews. Anderson (1998) suggests that most case study research in education is interpretive seeking to bring a case to life. He states that they often, but not exclusively, occur in a natural setting with the researcher employing qualitative and/or quantitative methods and measures as fit the circumstances. As Yin (2003) notes, the forms that the data collected will take essentially depend upon the nature of the particular case to be investigated.

In this way triangulation automatically takes place, thereby increasing the validity of the study. The collection of data in case studies also often involves colleagues who comment upon and discuss the research in the light of their own experiences. In action research case studies are felt to be more valid as a result of such scrutiny by fellow practitioners. Thus such case studies investigated by practitioner researchers contribute to the development of teachers as professionals.

A major criticism of case studies is that they lack representativeness of the wider population and, thus, researchers are unable to make generalizations from their findings. However, proponents claim the importance of the case study approach is the in-depth analysis and the understanding gained. For these researchers, the strength of this research approach lies in the 'relatability' of the findings (Bassey, 1990). By this term Bassey is suggesting that, although each case may be unique, there are sufficient similarities to make the findings from one study useful when seeking to understand others.

Three examples of case studies carried out by practitioner researchers are described in this chapter. The cases chosen are of different sizes but all take place within the respective teacher's school. The first looks at an issue, the use of teaching assistants, throughout the school. Here the school itself is the case. The second case study is of a small group of children within one class, whilst the third is of one individual pupil. The strength of such a research approach is that the teachers themselves are using a range of research methods to investigate a particular issue as it relates to them. Other teachers from the school are often involved and the research leads to discussion amongst the whole staff. It is important to remain cognizant of the very small-scale nature of these studies. The data were collected by these teachers during their working day. They would see themselves as novice researchers who were developing their skills and would be very loath to make overelaborate claims for their findings.

■ ■ ■ Case study: example 1

Summary

Title:
The use of learning support assistants, now known as teaching assistants, (LSAs) to support students with specific learning difficulties across the curriculum in a mainstream secondary school in the north-west of England.

Initial research questions:
1 What strategies are used to support students with specific learning difficulties in lessons?
2 How effective are these strategies for the teachers, the students and the learning support assistants involved?
3 How can we make more effective use of learning support assistants in this mainstream secondary school?

Methodology:
Questionnaires administered to learning support assistants.

Questionnaires administered to all staff.

Interviews of a sample of staff from a range of management and teaching responsibilities.

Interviews of a sample of learning support assistants.

Participant observation by the teacher researcher whilst working with learning support assistants.

Observation of a small sample of other teachers' lessons involving learning support assistants by the teacher researcher.

Findings:

These highlighted what the LSAs found difficult concerning their current practice in the classroom as well as what they saw as their strengths. They indicated the perspective of the staff concerning working with LSAs. From the findings the practitioner researcher was able to suggest future developments.

(A case study carried out by Amanda Isaac-Meurig.)

Discussion of case study 1

Amanda was a learning support teacher at a large secondary comprehensive school in the north-west of England. She worked with teachers throughout the school in all departments taking specific classes, withdrawing pupils and supporting subject teachers in lessons. She also worked with the LSAs, a relatively newly created group of adults, not trained as teachers, employed to support classroom learning. She felt that these LSAs had been introduced to the classroom in order to facilitate learning but that their role was very unclear to the teachers, the pupils and themselves. Amanda wanted to examine what was happening and also to explore the views both of LSAs and of teachers in order to initiate developments which would make more effective use of this extra adult resource in the classroom.

This is a case study of one school. The researcher identified the research questions and determined from these the respondents she wished to gather data from. Particular methods were then designed to do this. Questionnaires would enable data to be gained from all staff and allow them all the option of inputting their experiences and views, providing of course they wished to do so. More detailed accounts would be obtained from the interviews. These could be quite informal though conducted at pre-arranged times in specific environments, such as department offices, to allow for privacy and to avoid unnecessary distractions. Observations could be carried out during the respondents' daily support in lessons but several were arranged specifically to look at the use of LSAs by different teachers in their classrooms. This was perhaps the most difficult part of the data collection due to attempting to ensure some representativeness of the lessons chosen and to avoid observer effect.

The research focus was chosen because of the initial interest of the researcher. It was her experiences that identified this particular area of study. She was able to use her knowledge of the school to help identify the respondents quickly. She did not have problems in gaining 'access' to the staff and the fact that they knew each other helped in the carrying out of the data collection. All the staff, teachers and LSAs were told of the research and so the research process was open.

Findings

The LSAs noted that on occasions they lacked clear ideas about what was expected of them in the classroom and were unsure of the mainstream teachers' expectations. Although they knew in advance which lessons and teachers they would be supporting, LSAs still felt unfocused as they were often unsure of the curriculum content and the aims of the lesson. General 'helping out' also caused a degree of stress for the assistants as they often found themselves in classes where they were surrounded by students on the special needs register but were unable to give individual attention to everyone. In these cases, the LSAs tried to apportion time equally, but would have preferred more direct instruction from class teachers.

The research identified the use of LSAs as being effective in a variety of ways.

- Learning support assistants were most effective when they regularly worked with a variety of students within a class.

- LSAs were effective when providing incentives to learning and worked with individual students to set learning goals. It was widely felt by teachers and LSAs that having learners identify goals increased the probability that they would understand them and want to achieve them.

- Certain LSAs were observed giving frequent, early positive feedback that supported the students' beliefs that they could succeed with sufficient effort. This, in turn, helped students to perceive themselves as being valued members of the wider learning community within the school.

- The LSAs who held high but realistic expectations of the students in their care were most powerful in motivating reluctant learners.

- Effective LSA support encouraged students to focus on their continued improvement, did not emphasize past test results or make negative comparisons with other students.

- Many LSAs were quick to reward success and recognized sincere efforts even when the outcome was poor.

- Many of the LSAs observed were sensitive to the emotional needs of the students they supported and employed subtle strategies to alleviate learner anxiety.

The research also identified the following points as potential areas for development:

- Teachers are not always used to managing additional adults in a secondary classroom and, consequently, do not always take the initiative to motivate, delegate and manage the work of an extra adult in lessons.

- It might be beneficial for the Learning Development Department to implement an induction programme for new LSAs/teaching assistants (TAs).

- The LSAs/TAs need to be aware of the ways in which their roles may be developed and the importance of being up to date with changes in the curriculum and the effects of national strategies.

- With sufficient training, LSAs/TAs could make an active contribution to record-keeping and collecting evidence of students' achievements.

- When the timetables are set at the beginning of the school year, care should be taken to ensure that LSAs/TAs work in curriculum areas in which they feel confident.

- A number of LSAs/TAs requested more training in behaviour management techniques.

- Concerns remain about how to find time for the LSAs and teachers to plan and discuss lessons and the ways in which staff can be motivated to work collaboratively.

The findings were presented to the staff and the practitioner researcher was ultimately able to use these to help in the drawing up of a school policy on the deployment of teaching assistants that considered the future professional development of both teachers and teaching assistants.

This is an interesting case study carried out by a teacher in her own school. It has benefits in terms of developing the research skills of the teacher and involving other members of staff. It promoted discussion and raised awareness which ultimately led to changes in practice. We should also, however, be mindful of its limitations. This study is of only one school and, though this may be relatable to others, it is not possible to make generalizations from this single case. Here was one researcher who was researching the place in which she worked and, whilst she had knowledge of the school, she could also be biased due to social relationships formed over time. This may have affected how she saw and reported things. The fact that the staff knew about the research may have affected what they said to the researcher and their behaviour. However, the research was professionally relevant. It was conducted in an open manner and the data was scrutinized through discussion. As such it was likely to have a positive impact upon future practice.

■ ■ ■ Case study: example 2

Summary

Title:
Can working daily for a set period of time, in a structured learning situation, with a teaching assistant improve the skills of a specific group of pupils? A case study of one small group of reception children who are performing below their peers.

Initial research questions:
Can regular small group work with teaching assistants:

1 Significantly increase key word/letter sound recognition?
2 Encourage use of different reading strategies, that is, 1–1 correspondence, picture cues, initial letter cues, contextual cues?
3 Increase independent participation in whole-class teaching sessions?

Methodology:

Formal testing of identified group of pupils at both the start of the research and upon completion.

Teacher assessment of reading skills of pupils in this group.

Interviews with teaching assistant.

Observation of this small group of children working with teaching assistant.

Informal discussion between teaching assistant and teacher researcher of appropriateness of the activities and the daily format.

Findings:

All the children, who had been identified as falling behind others in the class, made significant progress, at least in the short term, when taught daily in a structured small group session with the teaching assistant.

(A case study carried out by Angela McGovern.)

Discussion of case study 2

The practitioner researcher was aware that in the early stages of their school lives some pupils were beginning to fall behind their peers. These children have no special needs requirements but have found concepts difficult to grasp and often needed additional explanation and support. The teacher felt that once pupils fell behind they found it increasingly difficult to participate in whole-class work. Therefore, it seemed essential to try to implement strategies as early as possible to prevent a wider gap being created and to develop the learning skills in these pupils so that they were able to 'hold their own' in full class sessions.

The teacher also wished to involve her teaching assistant more effectively in the learning process and decided upon a strategy whereby a small group of pupils (four) would be given, every day for 15 minutes, a preplanned (by both the teacher and teaching assistant together) structured session with the teaching assistant. It was hoped that this programme of small group work, held on a daily basis, would reinforce the pupils' skills and hold the children's attention much better than longer sessions held less frequently, perhaps once a week. It was hoped that their progress through these sessions would also make them more confident learners. Focusing on 15 minutes in this way would enable the teaching assistant to work with other children in the class for the rest of the day and so not see her monopolized by this small group. Activities were chosen from the National Literacy Strategy and a timetable was devised which specified the type of activity to be completed each day.

There was formal testing/measurement of keyword recognition and letter sound recognition at the start of the research and the children were assessed weekly and at the end to see progress made. Similarly the teacher assessed and monitored the development of the children's reading skills. Very short written evaluations were completed daily by the teaching assistant. These were used in the discussions between the teaching assistant and the teacher concerning the progress of the pupils which took place at the end of each week. In these weekly 'informal interviews' the appropriateness of the activities and planning for the next week also took place. The teacher researcher was able to observe the pupils working in a group with the teaching assistant. A pro forma of four questions concerning pupil activity and involvement was used to structure and record the observations. These are listed in Chapter 9 when looking at observation schedules.

Findings

The teacher researcher was very impressed with the results. At the end of the eight-week research period the children had improved in their ability to recognize keywords and initial sounds. Their reading strategies had developed as had their confidence. It would appear that in a short time the pupils had made rapid progress. Other classes in the school have also implemented the 'daily focused group' and they too were reporting significant increases in learning.

This was an interesting piece of research that the teacher wishes to develop further in the future. She does wonder what will happen to these pupils when they are no longer part of the focus group as will be the case when teacher attention moves to the next three or four pupils who now need this small group work. Will progress be maintained or will they regress? Also it would be interesting to know if progress would be maintained in the long term once the focus group was no longer seen as special by the whole class. Given our knowledge from the work of Vygotsgy (1962; 1978) on the impact of sociocultural experience on linguistic development, it is likely, of course, that all pupils could benefit in a similar way from such small-group work.

■ ■ ■ Case study: example 3

Summary

Title:
To evaluate the uses of different types of control technology in supporting the learning of one Year 6 boy with cerebral palsy.

Initial research questions:
What are the shortcomings in Peter's present curriculum?

In what ways is conventional control technology ineffective for Peter?

What type of software will make Peter's present curriculum more broad and balanced?

How will enabling technology open up paths to inclusion?

Will infrared control technology work for other children and should it become recommended practice for inclusion of pupils with physical disabilities in Year 7 in selected secondary schools?

Methodology:
Controlled experimental trials of different types of control technology.

Observation of Peter using the different forms of technology over time. Informal interviews with support assistant and also Peter's speech and language therapist.

Findings:

Two forms of control technology were found to be particularly beneficial to Peter in terms of making the curriculum more accessible. Both had different strengths and weaknesses and use of both in different combinations was seemed to be most effective.

(A case study carried out by Ray Elliott and Amanda Brand.)

Discussion of case study 3

Ray was a teacher in a special school for children with severe physical disabilities. It was hoped to include Peter, a pupil with quite severe athetoid cerebral palsy, into a mainstream secondary school in the following September. In order to make this possible Peter would benefit from being able to write unaided and so take a greater part in classroom learning activities. There had been a number of recent IT developments that could potentially help Peter in this. Ray hoped to trial these control technologies and to evaluate how they could benefit Peter. It was hoped that, subsequently, Peter and other pupils with similar learning difficulties would be able to benefit from this advanced technology.

■ ■ ■ The experimental approach

This third case study also uses what can be classed as a further research strategy, the experimental approach. The experimental method is often associated with positivist research (see Chapter 2). The experimental procedure involves the use of identical experimental and control groups that are kept separate. Whilst the control group is kept constant, specific variables affecting the experimental group are changed in particular ways and the subsequent developments are noted. Any resulting differences between the two groups can be assumed to be due to the changes made to the experimental group. Thus the effects of these variables on the subjects have been 'proved' experimentally. It should be possible to test the findings by replicating the experiment and obtaining the same results.

Experiments are a very useful way of carrying out research in the natural sciences. It is also possible to devise experiments on people though the participants may be unwitting. Thus psychologists may design experiments about certain aspects of learning or perception. However, it is difficult to consider whole classroom situations as becoming part of a traditional type of scientific experiment as there are so many variables involved that cannot be kept constant. The individual and unique nature of the human personality militates against the effective designation of control and experimental groups unless one uses characteristics such as age or gender. Teachers may be able to discern certain characteristics among particular age groups year upon year, however, the individuals who make up these teaching groups are not the same and they may be very different to teach. There are also important ethical concerns that arise from setting up experimental and control groups for experiments where classes and groups of children are concerned (see the section on ethics in Chapter 2). Thus in the social sciences experiments often take a very different form to those in the natural sciences.

A group of researchers at Birmingham University concerned with charting and improving classroom behaviour in the 1980s, advocated an experimental approach (Wheldall and Merrett, 1985). Instead of having a control group, their experiments established a baseline of behaviour through an independent observer (a teaching assistant or trainee teacher perhaps) recording aspects of pupil behaviour on an observation schedule. This is done at timed intervals and might, for example, be the number of occasions a particular pupil shouts out in a lesson or gets up from his seat. The teacher then introduces an intervention strategy designed to reduce the pupil's off-task behaviour. This is usually based on the provision of a reward such as credits or verbal praise. The observation is repeated after a period of intervention and the new data shared with the pupil. This is a straightforward research experiment, easy to implement if another adult is available. What is particularly interesting is whether any improvements in behaviour are sustained. This can be achieved by conducting a further observation at some distance in time from the intervention.

The experiment discussed here is taken from case study 3 outlined earlier. Ray and Amanda trialled different methods that Peter could use to write. Peter was taught to use the different methods. A 'fair' test was devised where he was set a task of writing his name. This was timed. These trials were carried out on eight occasions and the times noted (Figure 7.1).

Dates of trials etc.	Time taken to write 'Peter' with support from trained adult	Time taken to eye point 'Peter' using a headband and light pen on letter board	Time taken to eye point to word 'Peter' using a headband and light pen on word bank board	Time taken to type 'Peter' with Switch Clicker Plus on screen qwerty keyboard	Time taken to type word 'Peter' with Switch Clicker Plus on screen word bank	Time taken to type 'Peter' with Headway from Penny and Giles with on screen qwerty keyboard	Time taken to type 'Peter' with Headmouse from Don Johnson using Softkey
09/10/00	2 mins 45 secs	2 mins 07 secs	0 mins 22 secs	2 mins 32 secs	1 min 07 secs		
17/11/00		2 mins 03 secs	0 mins 24 secs	2 mins 39 secs	1 min 13 secs	3 mins 16 secs	
22/11/00		2 mins 11 secs	0 mins 21 secs	2 mins 41 secs	1 min 02 secs	3 mins 22 secs	
07/01/01		2 mins 09 secs	0 mins 22 secs	2 mins 28 secs	1 min 16 secs	3 mins 14 secs	1 min 25 secs
03/03/01		2 mins 15 secs	0 mins 23 secs	2 mins 36 secs	1 min 14 secs	Returned	0 mins 47 secs
12/03/01		2 mins 17 secs	0 mins 21 secs	2 mins 40 secs	1 min 06 secs		0 mins 32 secs
23/03/01		2 mins 21 secs	0 mins 25 secs	2 mins 35 secs	1 min 03 secs		0 mins 29 secs
02/04/01		2 mins 08 secs	0 mins 24 secs	2 mins 31 secs	1 min 03 secs		0 mins 17 secs

■ **Figure 7.1**

Research findings: Peter, Year 6

As shown in Figure 7.1 there is clear quantifiable data showing which method was quickest. This method was also the most susceptible to improvement in completion time as the trials progressed. This is a type of experiment where different methods of writing are used and the results measured. Every effort was taken to keep conditions constant. However, there is no control group, so we can only say these results apply to this pupil. Others with similar learning difficulties may score differently. It is fair to suggest though that these results give a reasonable indication of what technology would help Peter most and that this may be the same for other such pupils. Further tests on other similar pupils would help to show this. It is worth noting that further observations, informal interviews and discussions were used along with this experimental data in the final research report.

■ ■ ■ Conclusion

The examples referred to in this chapter should provide some ideas about how case studies and experiments might be used within practitioner research studies. As has been shown, the researcher must be alert to both the potential of such strategies to elicit data of interest to the project as well as to their shortcomings. In reviewing what has been learned from these examples, researchers might be encouraged to adapt such approaches to their own studies.

We turn next to two quintessential research methods, questionnaires and interviews.

■ ■ ■ Tasks: Developing an ethical approach to your research project

1. Use the BERA (www.bera.ac.uk) or ESCALATE (www.escalate.ac.uk) guidelines for ethical research to examine the research questions that you wrote at the end of Chapter 6. Identify any ethical issues to be addressed for each of the questions.

2. If you are studying in an HE institution, obtain a copy of their ethical guidelines for research. Discuss the policy of the institution and any procedures in place to monitor the ethics of research projects.

■ ■ ■ Suggested further reading

Gomm, R., Hammersley, M. and Forster, P. (eds) (2000) *Case Study Method: Key Issues, Key Texts*. London: Sage.

The editors have brought together a number of significant articles that discuss critically the case study approach. This is a text for the advanced practitioner researcher who wishes to read further about case studies as a research strategy.

Yin, R. (2003) *Case Study Research: Design and Methods*. 3rd edn. Thousand Oaks, CA: Sage.

This updated third edition provides a comprehensive guide to case study research. It discusses the importance of the case study as a research strategy and goes on to consider the practicalities of design, collecting evidence, analysis of data and reporting. This is a useful aid to practitioner researchers considering a case study approach.

■ ■ ■ Chapter 8

Questionnaires and interviews

■ ■ ■ Introduction

This chapter considers questionnaires and interviews as methods of gathering data. We outline how to design and conduct them and discuss the issues involved in using these techniques.

■ ■ ■ Questionnaires

When those new to, or unfamiliar with, the research process begin to think of gathering data from groups of people for research purposes, questionnaires are perhaps the method that immediately springs to mind. Pupils faced with a multitude of project assignments are a good example of this as they invariably resort to data collected via questionnaires. Parents, brothers, sisters and classmates are all potential respondents to a series of questions designed to generate evidence covering a wide range of subjects such as tastes in clothing, food, leisure activities, music and so on. A questionnaire is simply a list of questions that the respondents answer. It is clearly a useful method, if carefully planned, for gathering responses from a large number of people relatively quickly. As such, questionnaires may be seen as a useful means of obtaining quantitative data.

Data collected by pupils produces the sort of evidence that enables the construction of displays including charts and other graphical presentation. However, many teachers who have worked with pupils on designing and conducting questionnaires will be aware that a questionnaire which yields useful information is not as easy to design as one may think. A well-designed questionnaire can provide useful information on respondents' attitudes, values and habits. However, as is often the case with questionnaires designed by the inexperienced, the information gathered may not be that which the researcher is looking for. It is more difficult to obtain in-depth personal responses by this method and both questions and answers often remain superficial. It is because of this that qualitative researchers find questionnaires less useful. The danger for the inexperienced researcher is in reading an opinion into the data that is not substantiated by the questions. For example a politician who asks 'how do you rate our taxation policy on a scale of 1 (low) to 5 (high)?' may infer from an average response of 3 that the public are happy with the policy. However, respondents may actually have specific issues with the policy which the question does not allow them to express so they plump for a nondescript response rating. This example might just as easily be related to school cooks asking pupils to rate school lunches. Certainly the skills of the researcher are important when collecting data by questionnaire. Specific points need careful consideration.

Questionnaire design: key points to consider

The design of the questionnaire and wording of the questions are crucial to its success. Corbetta (2003) points out that the formulation of a questionnaire is a difficult task with no set of formalized precise rules for the researcher to follow. He does suggest, however, that the researcher needs to begin with a clear research hypothesis or focus and a knowledge of the population who will complete the questionnaire.

1.   *Reasons for using a questionnaire.* Researchers need to be clear about why they are planning to use a questionnaire to gather data. Whether this is an appropriate method or not will depend upon the type of information that needs to be collected to answer the research questions and the respondents it is going to be collected from. Questionnaires are useful in collecting a large amount of general data and opinions from a large number of people. However they are of far less use if you are collecting detailed information with subtle differences from respondent to respondent. Questionnaires tend to elicit responses that fit into broad categories with little opportunity for respondents to express complex emotional feelings in response to impersonal questions.

2. *Framing of questions.*

   (a) It is important to be clear about what information is sought from the questionnaire and to ask the questions that will yield the appropriate data.

   (b) Each question should have a purpose. Asking questions that are not needed is a waste of time and resources.

   (c) Questions need to be specific and the wording should be clear. Appropriate wording for the respondent group should be used, so wording of questions to Year 5 pupils on their experiences of the curriculum is likely to be different from a questionnaire asking for teacher responses.

   (d) The type of question must be decided upon, for example, you may want to ask pre-coded questions that offer a specific number of responses for the respondent to choose from. For instance, a researcher may ask respondents to tick the choice which best describes their approach to teaching RE, offering them descriptors such as 'multi-faith', 'anglo-centric', 'spiritual', 'humanist' and so on. Pre-coded questions are useful when it comes to collating the answers as they will all fall into one of a set number of categories. However we need to consider how appropriate it is to only offer respondents such a limited range of prescribed categories. Questions of this sort may begin to distort the data collected as respondents have to pick a category which is closest to how they would have answered if given a 'free' choice. For this reason the researcher may wish to ask open-ended questions where the respondent answers in their own words. These are useful in allowing a varied response. However, a wide variation of response makes these questions more difficult to collate. They also involve more commitment to filling in the questionnaire from the respondent and one danger is that respondents will give very brief answers just to finish the questionnaire. Thus asking a large number of open-ended questions may tend to put the respondents off and thus affect the quantity and quality of the data obtained.

   (e) In many questionnaires the names of respondents are not asked for, partly to ensure anonymity of respondents and partly because the sample size is so large that individual responses do not need to be identified. The preserving of the anonymity of the respondents needs to be considered very carefully. It may be that it would be useful to follow up respondents that have answered in a certain way later. Anonymity of response would rule this out.

3. *Collecting responses from questionnaires.* Though researchers want to collect data as a vital part of the research, many of the respondents may not share this interest and so will not be committed to completing the questionnaire. Traditionally many market research surveys are sent out by post. However, these have a notoriously low response rate. In education there is so much information sent through the mail that there is a tendency to deal only with those requiring urgent action and to 'file' the rest, sometimes in a nearby bin! In order to obtain as high a response rate as possible it is useful if the researcher can arrange to distribute and collect responses as this enables them to 'chivvy up' late responses. It is important to distribute at least twice as many questionnaires as are needed. This will allow for a level of non-response and in the unlikely event that 100 per cent are returned then so much the better.

Researchers need to have thought out a clear strategy in order to ensure a high return rate of questionnaires. Thus, if questionnaires are being distributed to all of the staff of a primary school, for example, it may be best for the researcher to arrange to collect completed questionnaires at the end of the day in person. This can be done without looking at individual responses and thus maintain respondent anonymity. However, in this case the researcher will be aware of who has not yet returned a questionnaire and so can arrange follow-up approaches over the subsequent days. However, if staff are asked to put completed questionnaires in a pigeon hole or a collection tray there is more likely to be a disappointingly low response. The researcher will need to resort to generalized appeals in staff meetings to an unidentified group of non-returners. It is worth reflecting on the efforts taken to ensure that the national census form, for which compulsory completion is backed by the force of law, are all collected in. This is done by a series of checks by the collection team whilst maintaining the confidentiality of the respondents' answers.

Questionnaire distribution to pupils can be a much more straightforward process if carefully planned. After all, pupils present a 'captive audience' to the researcher. Questionnaires can be given to whole groups of pupils at specific times, such as the beginning or ending of lessons, or during tutor periods, and can be collected in after they have been completed. Another useful point here is that the researcher can explain any general points to the class before they start and can answer specific individual questions during the filling in. In this way research students and teacher researchers can collect information from whole tutor or teaching groups in periods of just 25 to 30 minutes. If collected daily they can have responses from whole year groups by visiting a different tutor group per day for five or six days.

With questionnaires, the researcher must assume that the respondent has answered the questions in good faith. By being there as they are filled in by groups of pupils and by maintaining an appropriate atmosphere the researcher is more likely to ensure that this is the case. It is important that the atmosphere minimizes the potential for respondents to be influenced by researcher expectation and peer pressure.

An alternative way of administering the questionnaire is by the researcher reading out the questions to the respondent and noting down their responses. These are the researchers that we usually try to dodge in our local high street. The advantage for the researcher of this method is that they eventually reach the number of respondents required; however, it is time consuming and becomes a type of formal interview. Many teacher researchers have found that reading out the questions for pupils to answer on their own response sheets is a good way of administering questionnaires to whole classes. This is especially useful for mixed ability groups of pupils where some respondents may struggle to read the questions themselves.

Analysing questionnaires

If the planning has been done carefully then every question in the questionnaire will be there for a purpose. The aim is to elicit data that will help to address the major research questions of the study. With large

An example of a questionnaire

Excel College

Education Studies
Level Three

Module ED 3001: Investigating Educational Issues (2003/2004)

The purpose of this questionnaire is to gain information as part of our quality assurance procedures.

Your name (optional)

Please read each statement carefully and circle the response code which most closely corresponds to your own view.

SA = Strongly Agree, A = Agree, D = Disagree, SD = Strongly Disagree,
NA = Not Applicable/No View

AIMS AND OBJECTIVES

1	The module aims, objectives and forms of assessment were made clear	SA	A	D	SD	NA
2	There was considerable agreement between the announced aims and objectives of the module and what was actually taught	SA	A	D	SD	NA

TEACHING AND LEARNING EXPERIENCES

3	The tutor provided clear and useful sessions	SA	A	D	SD	NA
4	The tutor was accessible	SA	A	D	SD	NA
5	Each session had a clear purpose	SA	A	D	SD	NA
6	The module has stimulated my interest in the area being studied	SA	A	D	SD	NA
7	The module was delivered with enthusiasm	SA	A	D	SD	NA
8	Student contributions to sessions were encouraged and valued	SA	A	D	SD	NA
9	In the module I felt challenged and motivated to learn	SA	A	D	SD	NA

ASSESSMENT/OUTCOMES

10	Assessed work was interesting and stimulating	SA	A	D	SD	NA
11	The criteria for assessment were made clear	SA	A	D	SD	NA
12	Assessed work was returned within a reasonable time	SA	A	D	SD	NA
13	Tutorial support for assignments was useful and productive	SA	A	D	SD	NA
14	Feedback on assignments was helpful and constructive	SA	A	D	SD	NA

Continued over

SELF-EVALUATION

15 I attended all, or almost all, timetabled sessions	SA	A	D	SD	NA
16 I feel that I was able to make a satisfactory contribution to group discussions	SA	A	D	SD	NA
17 I found time to do adequate preparation for sessions/assignments	SA	A	D	SD	NA
18 I feel I have engaged with new/challenging ideas	SA	A	D	SD	NA

RESOURCES

19 Reading lists were specific and helpful	SA	A	D	SD	NA
20 Library books and journals were adequate for my needs	SA	A	D	SD	NA
21 Library staff were helpful and supportive	SA	A	D	SD	NA
22 Teaching accommodation (space and layout) was appropriate for the needs of the group	SA	A	D	SD	NA
23 Time allocated to the module was adequate	SA	A	D	SD	NA

QUALITATIVE REFLECTION
(Please feel free to continue answers to the following questions over the page)
24 What has particularly interested you in the module?
25 How could the module be improved overall?
26 How did you find the methods used?
27 How do you find the style of the tutor?
28 Any other comments?

■ **Figure 8.1**

Questionnaire to obtain student responses to a taught module as part of course evaluation

numbers of completed questionnaires it is a relatively mechanistic task to create a tally of answers for each pre-coded question. From this the researcher is able to present the overall responses to individual questions. This collation of data is rather more difficult with the more open-ended responses. Here the researcher may decide on a set of categories and place each response in one of these. The answers may then be collated and analysed as with pre-coded questions. There is an issue here of the researcher attributing meaning to the respondents' answers. An alternative method is to read through the open-ended responses noting each significant point. The end result is a list of main points mentioned in the responses and the number of times each was cited.

Once the data has been collated the researcher must then analyse it. This involves describing and explaining what the results show in relation to the respective research questions. Charts and graphs are often used to help express questionnaire results visually while statistical presentation describes the extent to which certain responses were significant. Statistical analyses using computer programmes such as SPSS are useful for dealing with large-scale samples. Having presented the data and/or analysed it statistically, the researcher has still to interpret what the data shows. Inevitably, any original hypotheses and relevant existing research will be used by the researcher to help make sense of the new findings.

The questionnaire in Figure 8.1 has been used by tutors for several years to evaluate student opinions of modules on a taught Education Studies course. The data was needed for a number of purposes. Tutors wished to know how the students had found different aspects of each module and their comments were genuinely useful in making improvements for future cohorts. They also needed to consider student responses for each module in order to write an annual subject report that had to be based upon firm evidence. Both the questionnaire results and the annual review were needed as evidence of course evaluation for the external inspection agency.

In this case a questionnaire usefully provided the sort of data required. There were responses on all the key areas that external inspectors examined and the internal annual report required. The information also gave a clear indication of what was enjoyed and found to be of use to students and that which perhaps was not and needed some attention. The questionnaires could be administered in the last taught session of each module; this ensured a high response rate. The students could fill it in reasonably quickly and so it was not seen as an onerous task and came to be viewed as part of the teaching process. Having five pre-coded choices for the first major section of the questions meant that the data could be quickly collated, even by someone who was not the actual lecturer. Currently, completed student responses are typed straight into a database by an administrator but in many universities students complete such questionnaires directly on line.

If students wished to expand their answers this could be done through the open-ended questions at the end. These open-ended questions were always the most difficult to collate as there could be quite a variation of response. However, they did tend to be negative in nature as 'happy' students were able to respond in the pre-coded questions and usually did not write anything in the open-ended section. Students who had an issue with anything in particular tended to expand on it in this last section. It was important when collating responses to record the comments as a proportion of responses to the questionnaire in general. These question-naires successfully achieved their purpose of providing student feedback on the modules. It was quick to collect and could be easily analysed. It should be noted that this questionnaire was only one means by which data was gathered on the teaching of these modules. There was also dis-cussion during staff/student committee meetings, informal feedback through individual tutorials and staff feedback through staff meetings.

Strengths of questionnaires as a means of data collection

1. It is possible to gather large amounts of data relatively quickly.
2. The researcher can compare the responses to particular questions from individuals or between different groups of respondents.
3. The data can be expressed statistically. It is thus possible to make comparisons with other studies (see Blaxter et al., 2001, for more information on questionnaire data analysis).
4. The research may enable overall statements to be made concern-ing the population, for example, the percentage who left school at 16, the percentage who gained certain qualifications, the numbers who felt that they were bullied at school.

Weaknesses of questionnaires as a means of data collection

1. Questions about complex issues are difficult to compose. Respon-dents may not find it easy to place their responses into specific categories.
2. The short responses often fail to reflect the varying depth or com-plexity of people's feelings.
3. It is the researcher who sets the agenda of questionnaires not the respondent. The questions may create attitudes by asking the respondents to comment on topics that they may not previously have considered. Alternatively, the questions may not give enough emphasis to issues that the respondents see as important.
4. The researcher may attempt to overcome such problems by adding open-ended questions. Answers to these will need to be codified

by the researcher and, to some extent, this can lead to the very subjectivity that the questionnaire had been chosen to overcome.

Oppenheim (1966) has written a classic text on questionnaire design and analysis. More recently Aldridge and Levine (2001) also give useful practical advice.

■ ■ ■ Interviews

The interview constitutes a fundamental research tool in the researcher's kit. Several important decisions need to be made in the planning of interviews concerning the form the interview will take, the role of the interviewer, how the data will be recorded and the final analysis. Interviews may take many different forms. They can vary from being highly structured and very formal to being unstructured and so informal as to appear as little more than conversations between respondent and interviewer (for a detailed overview see Bell, 1999, or Cohen et al., 2000).

Structured interviews

In the more structured interview researchers follow a set format asking fixed questions. How much they are able to adapt each interview to varying circumstances is decided beforehand but it may be very little. This approach allows for a team of interviewers to interview a large number of respondents and for the results to be standardized. This really is a further development of the questionnaire and is likely to provide quantitative as well as some qualitative data. The advantage this method has over straight questionnaires is that interviewers can clarify issues for respondents and they may be able to encourage the respondent to expand upon certain answers if desirable. The researcher can also note certain non-verbal responses that may help to illuminate answers further.

Unstructured interviews

A less structured approach is likely to be taken when the researcher wishes to place more emphasis on the respondent's own account, perhaps relying on a few fixed questions and prompts. The interview may be very informal and it may become, to all intents and purposes, like a 'normal' conversation. Here the discussion may be very open but the researcher must be careful not to lead the interviewees. These less structured interviews are more favoured by the qualitative researcher.

The most 'natural' interactions between the researcher and the respondent may take place during participant observation or a chance meeting whilst the researcher is conducting a case study (Hitchcock and Hughes, 1995, consider interviews in qualitative research in education). A teacher may take the opportunity to sit and chat to a pupil concerning an area she is researching into. The practitioner researcher needs to recognize that these 'chats' are informal interviews and can be a valuable source of data. Teachers actually carry out such informal interviews on a daily basis with a range of people such as parents, other teachers and teaching assistants as part of their work. Such data-gathering techniques could easily be used to collect data as part of a practitioner research project.

Selecting respondents

Interviewers must determine carefully who they wish to interview. For example, are the views of the headteacher more significant to the research question than those of a Year 7 pupil? Certainly the head has more power within the school, but it depends upon what is being researched. Burgoyne (1994) described what he called a process of 'stakeholder analysis' whereby he interviewed those who were identified as significant people, or postholders, in an organization in order to gain an understanding of how it operated on a day to day basis.

The interviewer must decide how to approach the interviewees since teachers, parents and pupils constitute very different interview groups. Teachers are constantly developing their interviewing skills, though they often do not realize this. They are used to asking questions in different ways and giving appropriate professional responses to the answers. They are aware of when it is appropriate, in a school context, to react in a way that shows delight, shock or annoyance. Thus an interview should be seen as a social interaction and teachers can exploit to good effect their skill at such interactions. Clearly, parents and pupils also develop questioning and responding skills though this is done within other contexts so they probably will not share the depth of educational understanding of the teacher and their constructs of schooling and learning may differ considerably.

Sometimes there may be a group of respondents who can be interviewed as a group, for example, a group of pupils participating in a particular class project that is being evaluated. This is known as a focus group (see Krueger, 1994, for a discussion of the effective use of such groups in research). They may be sitting together at a table and the practitioner researcher may ask them about the activity as a group. Feedback is obtained from the whole group and the results become refined through the discussion. This can be particularly useful when the research is concerned with future development as suggestions can be made by the project participants through this group discussion. The difficulty for the researcher is in knowing whether the group dynamics have affected the results in any significant way. The advantage of using focus groups is that larger numbers of respondents can be involved and are able to feel part of any classroom or school research project.

Interviewing skills

Research interviews share many of the features of interviews used in other contexts. For example, a training pack (LEAP, 1991) on conducting professional development interviews in the teacher appraisal process lists five key considerations:

- the quality and nature of questioning
- listening skills
- body language
- setting and atmosphere
- overall conduct of the interview.

These key issues are generalizable beyond professional development interviews and are thus applicable to research interviews. They can be elaborated as follows.

1. *Quality and nature of questioning.* The interviewer needs to be clear about what views/experiences she or he wants of the respondent and must ensure that all key areas are covered in the interview. The 'order' of the questions needs to be carefully thought out beforehand. For instance, the respondent is often initially put at ease with a number of 'routine' or introductory questions. The questions should be asked using appropriate language for the respondent and the interviewer must consider how to ask about sensitive issues. She or he needs to decide whether to keep questions on key areas together or to split them up and should be prepared for a range of possible responses having appropriate follow up questions ready.

2. *Listening skills.* Interviewers must not allow themselves to become distracted and should use verbal and facial signals to indicate interest in the responses. They should summarize briefly at intervals in the interview what the respondent has said to show that they are listening and also to check that they have noted responses correctly. If responses are being recorded by the interviewer, she or he needs to skilfully combine this with listening signals so that a relaxed conversational atmosphere is maintained.

3. *Body language.* The interviewer should consider the seating position of both the interviewer and interviewee and adopt an appropriate body position, open rather than closed. She or he should use appropriate eye contact and facial expressions to encourage when appropriate and to offer empathy in response to the interviewee.

4. *Setting and atmosphere.* The interviewer is usually the one to 'set up' the interview and thus has control over the setting and, by extension, over the atmosphere that she or he wishes to create. Consideration will need to be given to the timing of interview, the area in which it takes place and whether there will be refreshments. These things are important as they may make a significant difference to how an interviewee will react.

5. *Appropriate conduct of the interview.* The interviewer needs to treat the interviewee in an appropriate manner in order to elicit relevant information. Clearly, the conduct of a research interviewer is very different from that of a journalist interviewing a politician or

a police sergeant interviewing a suspect! By the end of the session the interviewee should feel good about the interview, comfortable that they have had their say and that someone has listened to them. The interviewer should close the interview appropriately and discuss any future meetings. It is important to return to interviewees where possible, to show them transcripts, perhaps discuss the interpretation, see if there is anything they wish to add, if anything has changed since and so on. Follow-up should also extend eventually to sharing findings with interviewees.

Clearly, then, it is important for researchers to hone their interview techniques and to be aware of how the quality of the data obtained depends very much on the interviewer (see Pole and Lampard, 2002, for a further discussion on conducting interviews). Interviews are an example of social interaction between people taking place in various contexts. Certainly research interviews have a power dimension to them of which the interviewer needs to be aware. Sometimes this is overt, for example, when a teacher interviews a pupil there is a clear status and power differential. At other times it can be more subtle.

When a newly qualified teacher (NQT), for example, has relaxed and informal interviews with her headteacher to explore school staff development issues, they are both aware that they are not of equal status in this situation and both act in their own interests. The interviewer should realize that a strategic approach in interviews is not just employed by the interviewers. It is useful to consider the work of Becker (1963) and also Goffman (1971) who analysed how individuals interpret social interactions in the light of their self-image and act as they see appropriate. This 'role-taking' also applies to interview situations.

Recording interview data

Interviews take many forms and they are tailored to suit each different research project. One of the most important decisions to be made by the researcher is how to record the data. There are several possibilities and both the interviewer and respondent need to be comfortable with whichever method is used.

1. *Making notes during the interview.* The researcher may opt to make notes whilst the respondent is talking. The difficulty here is in paying attention to the respondent and engaging in discussion whilst trying to write down the main points. Sometimes the flow of the interview becomes disrupted and there is a pause whilst the interviewer 'catches up'. This may make the whole interview more 'stilted' as the interviewee begins to concentrate on the ability of the interviewer to take notes. It is also difficult to get actual quotes from respondents as these take too long to write. The more structured the interview the less of a problem this is, as there is a clearer list of questions. Even in unstructured interviews the researcher will need to have an idea of what to ask about so will draw up an interview schedule, even if it is only a rough outline. There are many advantages of taking notes during the interview. The interviewer does not have to write up the interview later when they come to the analysis stage. She or he is also able to read back to the respondent, during the interview, what has been written in order to confirm that the meaning has been accurately recorded and that the main points have been noted.

2. *Tape-recording.* Some researchers prefer to tape-record interviews as this allows them to concentrate upon the interviewee and their responses. This is more often the case with unstructured interviews. Some researchers feel that tape-recording makes the interview more relaxed as both the respondent and interviewer are able to forget its presence once 'in flow'. However, some respondents do not wish to be taped when discussing certain topics, even if promised anonymity. Whilst one of the authors was interviewing teachers about staff appraisal sometimes the interviewees asked for the tape to be turned off if discussing a particularly sensitive aspect. As the Watergate affair showed in the USA, tapes can be more incriminating if they fall into the wrong hands, as voices can be identified. An advantage with tapes is that the researcher can play them back later. However if the interview lasts an hour then so does the tape and that can involve a great deal of time spent listening. Tapes ultimately have to be transcribed, either in shorthand notes or fully, and this can prove very time consuming. For full-time research teams transcribing such tapes can be a very expensive part of the research.

3. *Remembering and writing up later.* For very informal interviews and chance meetings there is often not the opportunity to make detailed notes or to tape conversations as they happen. Sometimes the briefest of points can be taken at the time. The alternative is to write rough notes down as soon as possible afterwards. If desired these can be confirmed with the respondent at a convenient time.

Analysing interviews

There are differing ways to analyse interview data and, ultimately, the researcher must feel satisfied that they have taken the meaning 'fairly' from the interviews. It is important that a series of issues/areas to be analysed have been addressed in each interview, usually stemming from the original research questions. The ease with which the data can be analysed is very much dependent upon how effectively they have been recorded. The researcher is looking for patterns that emerge through the interviews and any particular points of commonality or difference that need to be mentioned in the final report. This process of noting key points and linkages is usually termed 'codifying the data' and is usually done by the interviewer reading through the transcripts. Computer programmes have been developed that aid in this process by picking out key words and phrases in transcripts. However the researcher needs to be aware of problems that the software may have in deciphering meaning.

The final written analysis may be presented under a series of headings, related to the main research questions, with the researcher giving an overview of what the interviews have revealed. The reporting of a series of interviews often involves detailed description and can incorporate variations in the data, giving possible explanations for these. For further guidance on analysing interviews see Blaxter et al. (2001) and also Arksey and Knight (1999).

Discussion of an example of the use of interviews

The interviews (Figure 8.2) were carried out by a teacher as part of his research for a higher degree. The research was carried out in the mid-1990s after the introduction of the statutory appraisal of teachers. The

---

Title of research: Teacher perceptions and reactions to the introduction of performance appraisal: a case study of three comprehensive schools.

Consent of each school head was obtained.

Consent of all teachers to be interviewed was obtained. Two refused to take part.

A timetable for the interviews was drawn up on the basis of availability of interviewee and interviewer.

It was anticipated that interviews would last approximately 45 minutes each.

In-depth interviews were conducted with staff from different positions/posts at the three schools concerning their views and experiences of being appraised. Thirty interviews were conducted in all.

Designated interview room was made available and used in each school. Interviews were taped with the consent of each interviewee. One did not wish to be tape-recorded and so notes were taken during the interview with the respondent's agreement.

An interview schedule was used whereby certain questions about the interviewee were asked. These were designed to 'get the interview going'. Specific areas to be covered were listed as questions but respondents were allowed to 'talk around' the topic in their own way, questions being asked as appropriate and if a particular issue had not been covered.

■ **Figure 8.2**

An example of the use of interviews

researcher was interested in the effects of teacher appraisal and whether it was regarded by teachers as being beneficial for their professional development or as a threat to their personal autonomy. The sensitive nature of the whole process and the complexity and depth of different views meant that questionnaires were not an appropriate research tool. Neither was he able to use observation in the data collection process – it is not possible for a researcher to observe a supposedly confidential appraisal interview or an appraiser watching an appraisee teach without significantly affecting both situations. Thus interviews were chosen as the main form of data collection. These were to be in-depth interviews, and were to include staff who played different parts in the appraisal process from headteachers to NQTs.

Three schools were looked at as individual case studies. The schools were in the same small geographical area in which the researcher lived. He had worked at two of the schools as a teacher and also had close ties with the third. This could be seen as beneficial to the research as he was familiar with the schools and their staff. It made setting up the research easier. The interviews could begin with discussion of some common ground. The interviewer was familiar to the respondents and as such they were not talking to a stranger. Knowledge of the 'terrain' made it easier for the researcher to offer prompts and to probe certain issues when they seemed to be arising regularly. The interviewer gained a 'feel' for the appraisal process and how it varied in each school and this meant that in the later interviews he became more effective at 'getting to key issues for the interviewees'.

However, familiarity with the context can present dangers when it comes to choosing interview respondents. Assumptions may also be made which affect the nature of the interviews and how responses are interpreted. The preconceptions and prejudices of the interviewer need to be guarded against as much as possible.

Taping the interviews worked very well in this piece of research. A cassette recorder was used with a flat mike that lay on the table and did not have to be spoken into. This made it easier to conduct the interview as a conversation. Both parties were aware of the recorder but it did not overly intrude. The interviewer was able to listen and respond without having to worry about notes. Two interviews were lost due to technical breakdowns, that is, the batteries in the recorder were flat.

One member of staff did not want the interview to be recorded. The issue of teacher appraisal was very sensitive at the time. This respondent had some particularly strong views and felt that his voice could be identified in a recording whereas it would remain anonymous if views were recorded in note form. It is significant that two members of staff refused to take part at all. It would appear that they had particular views about either appraisal or experiences with senior management at their school and they refused to co-operate with anything that could be seen to be supporting the 'establishment line'. They took any research on appraisal to be colluding with an establishment position. The omission of such views can be seen to be important for this study. We see here the clear significance of who is interviewed and who is not. The aim must be to obtain a range of views. In this research this was attempted by taking a stratified sample, that is, interviewees from different levels of each school's hierarchy. Selection at each level was random but the representativeness of such a sample is always open to question.

It had been assumed that each interview would take approximately 45 minutes. In reality the times varied greatly. Some interviews lasted over an hour whereas others were finished in 15 minutes. Certainly the propensity to talk about their own teaching, professional development and appraisal, varied greatly from teacher to teacher.

Problems were created when some of the interviewees did not turn up. Often they had forgotten or sometimes they had to cover another lesson and so could not make the appointment. These interviews had to be rearranged or sometimes another teacher who was available agreed to take their place. Logistically this helped but it did affect the make-up of the sample.

Having accumulated many hours of interview on tape the contents were typed onto disk. This was a laborious process that was only accomplished with secretarial support. The researcher was then able to codify the transcripts straight from the disk copies. On return visits paper copies of the transcripts were shown to a number of the interviewees for them to check accuracy and to offer any further opinion. Also a critical friend of the researcher read through the transcripts and judged that the resulting analysis was fair. Consideration of the practical issues involved in this example may prompt researchers to anticipate similar concerns.

■ ■ ■ Linking of questionnaires and interviews

When considering triangulation, in Chapter 2, it was made clear that a mixture of methods is normally used in order to develop a greater understanding of practice. To illustrate how such a mix may work there follows an example of an investigation that initially used a questionnaire, which led on to the development of a series of in-depth interviews. The research was carried out as part of a master's degree dissertation and was an investigation into the monitoring and evaluation of the teaching of their subject by PE subject leaders.

The researcher, Steve Tones, was initially looking at how primary school teachers, who had been designated as subject leaders in PE, carried out this role. A questionnaire was designed to find out about the teachers' expertise in this area, how they felt about this responsibility and how they had set about fulfilling it. The data collected, when analysed, raised certain issues concerning the expertise of these co-ordinators, the priority of

PE within the curriculum and the time pressures placed upon subject co-ordinators. The researcher became particularly interested in a further issue that he picked up from the questionnaires. This was the difficulty these curriculum leaders had in monitoring the teaching of the subject across the school, in particular, how could they really make statements about the quality of teaching in PE when they were so busy teaching their own lessons that they could not see other classes taught? It was felt by the researcher that in-depth interviews with the subject leaders were now needed to look into this in more detail.

The questionnaire with answers from one of the respondents is shown in Figure 8.3. Then there is the interview schedule used by the researcher in which he intended to focus upon what the subject leaders saw as the strengths of PE in their schools and how these perceived strengths had been identified through monitoring and evaluation of teaching (Figure 8.4). This is followed by a system of codes that the researcher developed to interpret the interview transcripts (Figure 8.5). Finally, there is an extract from one of the interview transcripts with the codes written in by the researcher (Figure 8.6).

Steve's study provides a very clear illustration of how one method may lead to another as the researcher learns more about his area of interest and the potential and limitations of his chosen method to elicit the quality of data he desires. In Steve's case he realized that interviews would provide more in-depth quality responses, the questionnaire having provided the initial identification of significant issues. The responses were easy to collate but provided limited data on each respondent's subject leadership role and only facilitated a cursory explanation of the issues facing PE subject leaders. Steve realized from the responses to the final question that there was a great deal more to discover from these teachers and so devised some fairly in-depth interview questions. He maintained a good deal of structure in each interview as can be seen from the prompts and the detailed analysis via transcript codes. This was to ensure that the main issues were covered in each interview but also allowed some flexibility of response.

1   Are you the Curriculum Postholder for Physical Education at your school?

     [Yes√]   [No]

Academic/Education Profile: Please identify the following

2   University/College attended for teacher training

     Keele University   *Date: Sept 83-July 84*

3   Teaching qualifications gained

     P.G.C.E.

4   Main subjects(s) studied

     Geology

     Combined Sciences

5   How many hours were devoted to the teaching of physical education in your training?

     None

6   List any physical education/sport teaching coaching awards you have gained

     R.F.U.   *Preliminary Coaching Award 84*

     WRU   *Junior Coaching Award 95*

7   List all physical education in-service training courses attended (include dates)

     April 92 – Ball Skills
     Feb 95 – Gymnastics
     Sept 96 – July 97 C.A.S.E. Curr. Leaders

Teaching Profile

8   How long have you been teaching?

     13 years

9   Are you; (please tick one)

     class teacher   [   ]   teaching deputy head   [√]
     non-teaching deputy head   [   ]   teaching headteacher   [   ]
     non-teaching headteacher   [   ]

10   How long have you been the curriculum postholder for physical education?

     3 years

11(a) Are you a curriculum postholder for any other subjects?

     [Yes√] [No]

11(b) If Yes, list the subjects

Continued over

Science

12(a) Do you have any other additional school responsibilities?

[Yes√] [No]

12(b) If Yes, list the additional responsibilities

Pupil Discipline and Behaviour
School House Competition

Curriculum Role Profile

13 Why were you chosen for the position of curriculum postholder for physical education?

Knowledge of certain areas of the curriculum – games, athletics, swimming

14 Are you; (please tick one)

a leader of physical education   [√] or
a co-ordinator of physical education   [   ]

15 Do you have a clear written job description ?

[Yes√] [No]

16 Do you have additional financial allowance for this role?

[Yes] [No√]

17 Do you have teaching remission for this post?

[Yes] [No√]

18 Do you teach physical education to other classes?

[Yes√] [No]

19 How much physical education do you teach in an average weekly timetable?

4 hours

20(a) Have you written the policy for physical education at your school?

[Yes√] [No]

20(b) If Yes has the policy been implemented at your school?

[Yes√] [No]

21(a) Have you written a scheme of work for physical education at your school?

[Yes] [No√]

21(b) If Yes, has the scheme been implemented at your school?

[Yes] [No]

Continued over

22(a) Have you written units of work for physical education at your school?

[Yes] [No√]

22(b) If Yes, are any units used by other teachers?

[Yes] [No]

22(c) List the units used by other teachers

23 Have you offered advice and guidance to colleagues about teaching physical education?

[Yes√] [No]

24 Have you taught physical education alongside other colleagues?

[Yes√] [No]

25(a) Do you organize the extra-curricular physical education activities?

[Yes√] [No]

25(b) Are you responsible for each extra-curricular physical education activity?

[Yes√] [No]

5(c) List the extra-curricular physical education activities you are responsible for.

Soccer Rugby Rounders Athletics

26(a) Have you provided any in-service training for colleagues in physical education?

[Yes√] [No]

26(b) If Yes, list the training you have provided for colleagues.

Games – Ball Skills
Dance – General

27(a) Do you monitor the teaching of physical education across the school?

[Yes] [No√]

27(b) If Yes, is the monitoring effective?

[Yes] [No]

28 When do you communicate ideas about the teaching of physical education to other colleagues?

Staff meetings

29 Who would you identify as being the most help to you in your role?

Headteacher

30(a) Are there any barriers limiting your effectiveness in your roll?

Continued over

[Yes√] [No]

30(b) If Yes, list in order of importance any barriers to your effectivness

1 *No non-contact time to observe lessons*
2 *Reluctance of colleagues to change*
3 *Other subjects needing attention*

30(c) What strategies you have used to overcome these barriers.

1 *Providing specialist teaching in certain areas of activity eg swimming, gym, dance*
2 *Prioritizing attention to diff. areas of the curriculum*

Please comment on any other information or issues that you wish to highlight concerning your role as a curriculum postholder for physical education.

The biggest issue I feel is the size of classes measured against the resources available e.g. Large Class (35) in a small school hall for a Gym Lesson and also the low priority given to P.E. in the Primary School; because of the attention given to the core subjects most teaching staff feel P.E. is not that important in terms of the overall primary curriculum.

■ **Figure 8.3**

Curriculum postholder for physical education questionnaire

What are the strengths/limitations of PE at your school?

Prompts
Standards in teaching – different activities

Standards in pupils' learning – different activities

Other features of the PE – extra curricular work – resources – timetable

How have you found these things out?

Prompts
What monitoring strategies were used?– observation – discussion – meetings – questionnaire – plans – video

What did each approach focus on? – teaching approaches, class management features, quality of pupils' movement, organization, task setting

Who monitors? (persons) – subject leader – another teacher (buddy) – headteacher – PE adviser

What is the timescale for monitoring – opportunity – regularity

Is there a structure, policy, agreed format?

What is the extent of monitoring? – selective – across the key stage

How are the outcomes recorded?– notes, video

What happens to the information post monitoring and evaluating?

Prompts
A written/verbal report?

Who sees it? – teachers, head, shared with others

What happens next? – target setting – action plan – LEA framework

What are the advantages/disadvantages of this whole process?
Prompts
Raising standards – progression
Issues – time – conflict – power – responsibility

■ **Figure 8.4**
The final interview schedule

Category:

Monitoring methods or approaches/M

Sub categories for monitoring methods

audit/au q/questionnaire
observation/ob st/structured us/unstructured
discussion/di f/formal time if/informal time
reading/re
teaching alongside colleague tac
assessment of pupils/ap

Category:

Evaluation statements or comments/E

Groups:

strengths of PE/st
limitations of PE/li

Sub-categories for evaluation statements:

teaching/te
pupil learning/pl
content and structure of PE/cs
extra curricular activities/xa
resources/res

Category:

Action planning/AC

Sub-category for action plan

INSET/in
resources/res
assessment of pupils/ap
content and structure of PE/cs

Category:
Issues/I

Sub-category for issues

time/ti
resources/res
financial/fi
content and structure of PE/cs

▦ **Figure 8.5**

The transcript codes

ST	Tell me about the strengths of PE at your school?
VP	We all obviously teach our own class – I like the way we do sports day – **E-St-te** it's not a competitive thing, it's a personal challenge day – where they are personally challenged rather than racing somebody else – **E-St-te** you know it is how well they can do – their personal best – I like that. I think that is a strength – **E-St-pl**
	They have a lot of people coming in and helping which is nice from the local College – people coaching for tennis – **E-St-te** we also have visitors – dance and things – which have been quite good – **E-St-te**
ST	Advisory?
VP	People like the Indian Lady – Indian dance – not really advisory – we have had training which is a little different – **E-St-te**
ST	Limitations?
VP	Limitations for the staff or generally the school – well we would like to do more outdoor activities – as younger children – we are sharing space at the moment – with the nursery – I reckon that money is always a problem – because we always want more resources – **E-li-res**
	We are always losing balls – always start with six balls at the start of the half term – and we never have any at the end
ST	Standards of teaching!
VP	I wish I could tell you to be honest – well I work very closely with my other reception class teacher – and we do very much similar things and she has kind of picked up one or two things that I have done – **M-tac** which worked well- **E-St-te**
ST	How has she picked up on these things?
VP	Well, we plan together – and say what did you do – so we work quite closely together – **M-st**
ST	And have you seen her teach?
VP	I have seen her teach but not watched a whole lesson – I haven't seen any of the teachers teach a whole lesson – **M-ob**
ST	But have seen them teach for some parts of lessons?

VP	Only by looking through the hall – I don't actually watch them – **M-ob-us**
ST	What's your general impression?
VP	Very controlled – quite good – I would say – **E-St-te**

Note: *VP is the teacher and ST is the researcher.*
This example is from a master's dissertation entitled 'An investigation into the monitoring and evaluation of PE subject leaders' by Steve Tones.

■ **Figure 8.6**

Extract from an interview transcript

Strengths of interviews as a means of data collection

1. It is a research method that is adaptable to different situations and respondents.

2. The interviewer can 'pick up' non-verbal clues that would not be discernible from questionnaires, for example, the annoyance or pleasure shown by the respondent over certain topics.

3. The researcher can 'follow hunches' and different unexpected lines of enquiry as they come up during the interview, for example, issues of bullying may become apparent that had not been mentioned or suspected before the start of the study.

4. The interviewer can collect detailed qualitative data expressed in the respondent's own words.

Weaknesses of interviews as a means of data collection

1. The interviewer may significantly affect the responses by inadvertently influencing or leading the respondent.

2. Interviews can take a great deal of time and may be difficult to set up. This inevitably restricts the number it is possible to carry out.

3. The more unstructured the interviews are then the more variation there is between interviews. The 'uniqueness' of each interview makes collating the data more difficult.

■ ■ ■ Conclusion

In reviewing the use of questionnaires and interviews through the presentation of examples the reader can see both their utility and their drawbacks. Each is capable of eliciting important data but the quality of the outcomes is dependent upon how well the researcher crafts and deploys their chosen tool. There is a great deal more that researchers can learn about these two fundamental techniques through accumulated experience of their application. We now proceed to look at observation as a further important research method.

■ ■ ■ Task: Designing a questionnaire and an interview schedule

1. Choose one of the research questions that you wrote at the end of Chapter 5. Design a questionnaire to gather data on this research question. Pilot the research tool with three respondents (these could be members of your research group). Evaluate the research tool that you have designed and amend it as appropriate.

2. Choosing another of your research questions, design an interview schedule to gather data. Conduct a pilot interview (this could be with a member of your research group). Evaluate the research tool that you have designed and amend it as appropriate.

■ ■ ■ Suggested further reading

Aldridge, A. and Levine, K. (2001) *Surveying the Social World*. Buckingham: Open University Press.

All aspects of social survey research are addressed in this book. There is a detailed discussion of the design and conducting of questionnaires and structured interviews followed by sections on the presentation and analysis of data.

Arksey, H. and Knight, P. (1999) *Interviewing for Social Scientists*. London: Sage.

This book explores the use of interviews in social research. It considers the design, conducting, recording of data and analysing of interviews in a variety of contexts. Practitioners will find this text very helpful when considering this method for their own research.

Drever, E. (1995) *Using Semi-Structured Interviews in Small-Scale Research: A Teacher's Guide*. Edinburgh: Scottish Council for Research in Education (SCRE).

This is a companion text to that on questionnaires by the same author. It is, likewise, a good practical guide for teachers thinking of employing this particular research method.

Munn, P. and Drever, E. (1995) *Using Questionnaires in Small-Scale Research: A Teacher's Guide*. Edinburgh: Scottish Council for Research in Education (SCRE).

This is a short text on the design and conducting of questionnaires. It is a good practical guide for teachers thinking of employing this particular research method.

■ ■ ■ Chapter 9

Observation

■ ■ ■ Introduction

This chapter considers the important part that observation plays in the research process. How to structure observation and gather data from it are discussed in detail. The strengths and weaknesses of the method are outlined and the chapter concludes by linking observation with other methods of data collection.

■ ■ ■ Observation as a research method

We spend much of our lives observing what is going on around us. We 'weigh up' situations as we observe them and our resulting actions are based upon data gathered from these observations combined with what we have previously observed and interpreted. Thus observation is an important means by which we come to understand our world. For our research purposes, the type of phenomenon to be observed and the perspective of the observer will be key factors in determining how we actually organize and carry out the observation.

Observation can take many forms. It may be formal and overt as in many psychological experiments where the researcher notes the reactions of respondents to certain stimulations. Similarly, OFSTED inspectors at the back of a classroom with their clipboards are observing the lesson formally and overtly. Observation may also be formal and covert with those being observed unaware of the observer. Here the 'action' may be observed through closed-circuit television (CCTV) cameras, two-way mirrors, or the observer may be hidden in the crowd. The observer may take part in the proceedings with the subjects of the observation sometimes aware that they are being observed and sometimes not. Thus a teacher researcher may 'help' in another teacher's classroom whilst unobtrusively observing. In our earlier case study examples a teacher was able to observe whilst giving special needs support to pupils in different classrooms (p. 88); another was able to observe, unnoticed, a group of pupils working with a teaching assistant (p. 91). These teacher researchers did not want to disrupt the 'normal' situation and thus continued to carry out their 'usual role'. On the other hand, Ray Elliott and Amanda Brand (p. 94) were able to watch and record the use of different IT equipment quite openly, confident that they were not influencing the results.

Thus observation varies in its formality and openness. It may yield certain amounts of quantitative data or it may concentrate on qualitative descriptions. Much depends upon how the observation is designed by the researcher and this is, in turn, dependent upon the type of activity being observed. The observer can affect the situation in many ways and awareness of this influences the design. Certainly it would be difficult to put the case that observation by OFSTED inspectors does not affect the performance of teachers at all. Also the visiting and observing of lessons by headteachers may not just be for gathering data on teaching and learning in the school, but may also be part of the regular processes that emphasize their authority. Thus, as with other research methods, there are power implications in the use of observation and in the way it is conducted. Montgomery (1999) notes how the setting up of a teaching observation programme within a school can be seen in very different ways by the teachers involved, depending upon how the whole process has been set up and who has ownership.

Teachers are very skilled at making observations, perhaps without even being aware that they are doing so. Observation is built into their training and they have developed the appropriate skills in order to aid their teaching. Teachers are well aware of the problems caused by not being sensitive to certain developments in the classroom. The regular scanning of the class is second nature to an experienced teacher and the ability to spot the early signs of pupil restlessness or inattention is well developed. However, whilst certain things are noticed on a daily basis by teachers in their lessons, others are not really looked for and may be totally missed. For the purposes of research and data collection we need to reconsider observation techniques in more detail.

In setting up observations the researcher must be sensitive to the situation. It is clearly inappropriate, for instance, to use overt formal observation methods when researching the counselling of pupils by teachers. Neither is it possible to observe some situations without having a drastic effect on the outcome, for example, a researcher observing a head of department conducting a staff development interview with an NQT is likely to have at least some impact upon how the interview is conducted and the interaction that takes place. Other methods of data collection may be considered more appropriate in these examples.

What researchers need to do when conducting observation is to consider their ethical position. Observing can in some situations be regarded as a form of snooping so the teacher researcher has to consider who needs to be aware that the observation is taking place and what its purposes are. The researcher also needs to consider the involvement of other staff. Certainly for any adult working in a classroom to find out that they had been observed even indirectly by researchers and fellow teachers, and that some record had been kept without them having been informed, is likely to significantly damage future working relationships with colleagues. Some researchers would suggest that observing pupils is part of the everyday teaching process and therefore pupils do not need to be informed. This may be the case but pupils do have human rights which should be taken into account along with the need to obtain parental consent. Thus, whilst observation is a very useful means of gathering data on what is happening in classrooms, the researcher needs to be continually sensitive to the ethical issues.

The techniques employed in the collecting of data are very important in this approach. The observer may be openly noting events as they occur or they may have to remember them to be written up as soon as possible afterwards. The more formal the observation the more detailed a tally chart that is devised resulting in a high yield of quantitative data to be analysed. With the more informal observations the schedules become looser in outline until, in full participant observation, the observer is making mental notes under broad headings to write up later.

However, it is impossible to observe and note down everything that occurs in a complex situation such as a classroom of 25 children and one or more adults. The researcher needs to plan and structure the observation on the basis of what it is they are looking at. The extent to which the observation is tightly structured will invariably depend upon whether quantitative tallies of certain behaviours are sought as opposed to looser descriptions of events.

Often researchers may carry out open or unstructured observations in the very early stages of research in order to familiarize themselves with the topic. These initial observations may raise issues they had not considered or to help to further refine their research questions. They often prove valuable in the designing later of more structured observation schedules.

Examples of observation schedules

Schedules displaying the most clearly defined structure are presented first in the following examples, moving on to those that are more open.

Classroom layout and pupil participation

The classroom layout in Figure 9.1 will be familiar to any teacher, pupil and parent. Plans such as these form the basis of initial observation and analysis. Using these a researcher is able to chart individual pupils' participation over time and can then consider influences such as ability, gender and behaviour. They can also capture data about how the teacher actually controls or influences interactions through seating comparing different classroom layouts. The researcher is able to use letters, numbers or some such symbol to show particular activities related to pupils and where they are sitting, such as which pupils volunteer answers to questions, who the teacher asks, or who does not contribute in whole-class discussion sessions. It is also possible to chart teacher and pupil movement around the room in relation to such mapping.

In these situations the researcher needs to have the ability to identify particular behaviour/actions and to record them quickly. There may be a question of classification here, for instance, in deciding which category a particular action falls in. The more categories behaviour is to be recorded into the more detailed the observation becomes but the more difficult it is to actually record. Thus whole-class observation, by necessity tends, to be more general in nature. However the observer may focus on one pupil or a small group. It is also difficult to record absolutely everything as it is impossible to write continuously and observe at the same time. In many classroom observations this is overcome by scanning

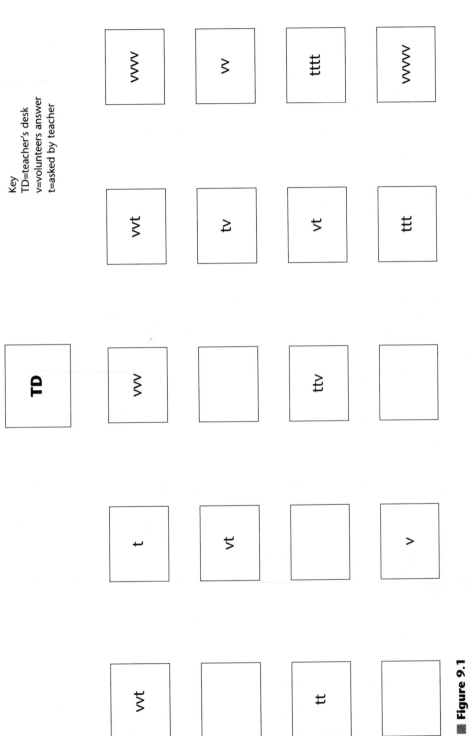

■ **Figure 9.1**
Pupil participation within a traditional classroom layout

	Peter	Mary	Joanne	Aftar	Dean
1st scan					
2nd scan					
3rd scan					
4th scan					

■ **Figure 9.2**

Small group scan

those individuals or groups being observed at specific intervals. This may be every minute, every three minutes or five minutes and so on. The time depends upon the observer's decision as to appropriateness.

Small group scan

Here the researcher may wish to note numbers or letters for particular activities for each child, for example, 1 for reading, 2 for writing, 3 for talking to another pupil apparently on task, 4 for talking with another pupil apparently off task, 5 for working with teaching assistant. These numbers can be filled in for each pupil per scan (Figure 9.2). Or a brief description may be written in each such as 'playing with marker pen'.

These classroom observation schedules have been derived and modified from original examples given by Hopkins (2002) but variations have been used for some time by other researchers (see, for instance, Wheldall and Merrett, 1985).

The teacher researcher may wish to focus on individuals within a learning situation. Here the observation may be more detailed as the following examples illustrate.

Individual pupil observations

Figure 9.3 is an example adapted from a detailed study of one child carried out as part of an investigation by a foundation degree student. The aim of such a detailed investigation is to develop an understanding of how children operate on a day-to-day basis in an early childhood setting. This student carried out a number of observations using the schedule below. This enabled her to develop a picture of the child's daily activities which could be added to data collected from a number of other sources such as conversations (interviews) with the child, other adults in the nursery and her parents. For further discussion of the importance of observation in learning about young children and examples of how to develop suitable observation schedules see Fawcett (1996).

NAME: Olivia   **AGE:** 2 years 3 months   **GENDER:** Female
DATE: Thurs. 8 Jan. 2004   **OBSERVATION:** 1

AIM: To observe a child's interaction with others in a nursery setting.

	9.30 a.m.	9.45 a.m.	10.00 a.m.	10.15 a.m.	10.30 a.m.	10.45 a.m.	11.00 a.m.	11.15 a.m.	11.30 a.m.	11.45 a.m.
Participation in classroom activity										
Child not involved in any activity										√
Child plays alone			√	√				√	√	
Child plays with others		√			√	√	√			
Talk with others										
Child plays silently							√	√		
Child plays talking to self			√	√					√	
Child talks with others		√			√	√				
Initiates conversation with adult										
Responds to adult	√									
Summary	Olivia seemed happy and content playing on her own, joining in with others when asked and when she wanted to contribute									

■ Figure 9.3
Observation of one child's interaction in a nursery setting

The chart in Figure 9.4 was used by a researcher whilst observing the teacher and two identified pupils over a 60-minute period in a lesson (see research by Linda Rush in Chapter 11).

■ ■ ■ Small group observation

In Chapter 7 a case study was outlined in which Angela McGovern studied the progress of a group of four pupils working with a teaching assistant.

School *******		Subject/topic **English**	
Teacher *******		**Date/time** 17.3.03 9.15 a.m	
Class Y6			

Teacher	0	Pupil 1 Alistair	0	Pupil 2 Richard
Listening to Rosie reading homework		Finishing off		Listening to Rosie – Watching Alistair
Praising Rosie – asking Ainsley to discuss Rosie's writing		Discussing Rosie's writing and listening to next person		Listening to next person
Discussing words used in girl's writing		Listening and joining in discussion		Listening and joining in discussion
So many different ways of saying 'said'		Listening to teacher and class and individuals reading		Hands up to indicate that he read his writing out to someone at home
Writing notes re: child's reading of their writing	10	Listening to teacher praising child and importance of indirect speech	10	Listening –
Discussing with children how useful it is to pick up from others		Listening – receiving book.		Listening and receiving book
What page are we on Rebecca? Briefly, Hayley, tell us where we are up to		Hands up to offer his summary so far		Looking at text – listening to teacher
Reading of chapter – do you want to carry on Richard		Following text		Following text – reading of text
Thank you Richard what's Mum doing, how did the Author describe the......		Listening to discussion		Reading of text – listening to discussion
What would be the opposite of chickening out?	20	o.t./listening	20	Listening to other children's ideas
Let's find out what happens – Reading of text		Following text		Following text
Anyone like to make some sort of prediction here?		Listening to other children's ideas		Listening to other children's ideas
Listening		Reading of text 'it seemed – where's that?'		Listening
OK thanks Alistair well done. Reading of text		Listening to teacher reading		Listening to teacher reading
Reading text. What's he doing?	30	Listening/following text	30	Listening/following text
Reading text		Listening/following text		Listening/following text
Reading text		Listening/following text		Listening/following text
Reading text		Listening/following text		Listening/following text
Reading text - questioning		Listening/following text		Listening/following text
Phew! Why is Helly cheered up now by Kitty's story?	40	Listening/following text	40	Because she had the same problem with toadstools
With partner/gps think of 10 major incidents that happened in book		Listening to instructions		Listening to instructions
Chatting with individuals. Do it chronologically. What does that mean?		Sat by Richard. Discussing with one another		Sat by Alistair. Discussing with one another.
Talking to me		Discussing/writing/looking through book.		Discussing/writing/looking through book.
Observing – standing back		" " "		" " "
Prompting children – you might come up with more than 10 priorities	50	" " "	50	" " "
With a pair/table groups		" " "		" " "
Rotating round tables????		" " "		" " "
A lot of you should have same ones – but there is a gp with an important one		" " "		" " "
With Alistair and Richard		" "		" "
Asking children to collect resources/books in	60	Finishing – handing in work	60	Finishing – handing in work

▪ **Figure 9.4**

Full lesson script with more able pupils

This group worked together for 15 minutes every morning for eight weeks. Angela was able to observe the group unobtrusively for a number of sessions and though the teaching assistant was aware that she was observing the children working, the pupils were so used to having both adults in the vicinity that they did not notice her observing. Angela used what she termed semi-structured observation in her research. The observation schedule consisted of a series of four questions (Figure 9.5), under which she was able to write notes concerning individual pupils and the group as a whole during and immediately after the observation.

How do the children participate? (e.g. eagerly, voluntarily, need to be
   questioned)
Is there evidence of the children using reading strategies?
Are the activities suitable/suitably paced for the needs of the children?
Do the children concentrate for the entire session?
(Observation schedule used in research by Angela McGovern)

■ **Figure 9.5**
   Observation schedule of interaction of pupils with teaching assistant

A further example of observation carried out by a teacher researcher also involves a relatively open observation schedule on which data were collected during the observations based on a number of headings.

> The focus of each guided writing observation was to observe the role of the teaching assistant, the type of support given, what was actually taught about writing and the reaction of the six children during the activity. Detailed notes were taken describing the conversations, questions and answers between the six identified children and the teaching assistant. (Claire Realff, 'A study examining strategies used to raise standards in writing in an early years setting').

These observation schedules are the means by which the researcher is able to order and collect data appropriate to the focus of study. As with all other methods, observation provides the evidence that enables us to analyse and make judgements about what is happening in different situations. However, we must not take data to be reified as the 'truth' about what is happening. The researcher has to make judgements throughout the process concerning when to observe and when not to, what is observed and recorded and what is not, which actions fall into the different categories and so on. The researcher interprets what is seen in the recording process even as it is happening as well as during the data analysis stage later.

■ ■ ■ Analysing observations

Observations have usually been designed to gather data on a number of specific issues. In analysing the findings the researcher needs to examine them on each of these issues in turn. For instance, a schedule may have been designed for observing a group of pupils working in a lesson. The schedule will perhaps show over a number of scans what each pupil was doing in terms of a number of behaviours such as working silently, talking to other pupils, walking around the classroom. The data can be summarized for each of the pupils observed and from this an overall account constructed of the behaviour of the whole group in the lesson. Repeated on a number of occasions the analysis will show behaviour over time of individuals and the group as a whole. The ease of analysis of observations is very much dependent upon how they have been recorded in terms of focus and detail.

■ ■ ■ Linking observation to other methods of data collection

As with questionnaires and interviews, observation is often used in combination with a range of other methods of data collection. There follows a case study that uses a combination of interviews alongside observations.

Case study

Title:
An exploration of the strategies teachers and teaching assistants can employ to intervene in children's play and the effect that these strategies have on the learning that takes place.

Initial research questions:

How do adults and children feel about play?

How do adults and children feel about intervention in play?

How do children play when they play alone/before adult intervention?

How do teachers and teaching assistants currently intervene in pupils' play?

What different forms of adult intervention could be used?

How does play change with different forms of adult intervention?

Methodology:

Observation of children's play before adult intervention.

Observation of adult intervention in play and its effects upon the play.

Informal interviews/discussion with staff and children about play.

Findings:

'Distance' intervention, or intervention led by the child appeared to be the most effective for learning. When adults led play from the start and had their own clear ideas of outcomes the play was often less inventive and inspiring.

(Carried out by Carole Owens.)

This teacher researcher felt that the whole area of early years education had undergone rapid change with the development of the foundation stage. She was aware that children were now starting school at a far earlier age than in previous years and that schools therefore needed to provide an appropriate curriculum. She wanted to examine play as a vehicle for children's learning and specifically the effects of adult intervention in supporting learning through play.

She wanted to observe the effects of three different strategies for intervention.

1. 'Distance' intervention whereby the children are given information or ideas for play away from the setting itself, for example, through story sacks.

2. The adult is present but intervention is at the child's request.

3. The adult takes an active role in the play from the outset.

The practitioner researcher spent several 'practice' sessions, observing the children at play to get used to the technique of observation, and also to focus afresh on how children were playing in the classroom situation rather than relying on her pre-formed opinions based upon previous experience.

In the actual research project, several 20-minute observation sessions of each strategy were carried out on two identified groups of children, although other children did sometimes enter the play. Since motives for certain play behaviour could only be inferred from the observations, informal interviews/discussion were held with staff and the children to gain some insight into their feelings about play, adult intervention in play, time spent playing and so on. The other reception class teacher and the two teaching assistants thus also became actively involved in the research.

The teacher researcher was aware that her findings were very tentative due to the very small-scale nature of her research and the limited amount of data collected initially. This was the teacher's first piece of research since leaving college many years previously. She did say that carrying out the observations had taught her a great deal that she had not realized about the children and how they play. The research had also reawakened in her an interest in the current literature on play and early years development that she was continuing to read. Some of the actions that emerged from the research were for the staff to continue to work closely together, to observe pupils carefully, to discuss their practice and to share ideas as part of continuing professional development. Thus the overt use of observation in this case led to a greater awareness among a group of teachers about the differential impact of these pedagogic strategies.

◼ ◼ ◼ Strengths of observation in data collection

1. It is possible to see how people behave in 'natural' situations, for example, watching pupils play.

2. The researcher can see whether the subjects in the observation act as they say they do.

3. An observer can gather large amounts of data in a short time, for instance several lessons can be observed in one day.

4. Observations may bring certain practices and behaviours to the

attention of the practitioner researchers of which they had not been previously aware.

■ ■ ■ Weaknesses of observation

1. Gaining access to situations that would be useful to observe can prove difficult, for example, bullying usually takes place secretively and away from adult eyes, and outside observers are not normally allowed into sensitive or confidential discussions.

2. It is difficult to observe and record at the same time, for example, some observation schedules require recordings to be taken every few seconds.

3. Sometimes it is difficult to categorize behaviour into the predetermined codes on the schedules, for example, deciding if pupils talking is on-task or off-task behaviour.

4. The observer may affect the situation as is frequently the case when a school inspector is viewing a lesson.

5. There are ethical issues of observing people if they do not know that they are being observed. It is also difficult for a teacher observer not to intervene if they feel it is warranted by events.

■ ■ ■ Conclusion

Observation is a very efficient method of research and can lead to greater understanding. It is important, however, to always keep in mind the human processes by which the data is gathered when evaluating and making use of the findings. It is not always possible to understand actions by observation alone, for example, why a teacher is treating children in a classroom differently. A follow-up interview may be needed. This may turn what is initially perceived as a weakness in the method into a strength by providing a fuller analysis, which ultimately improves the depth of the whole research project. In the next chapter we look at the potential of extant documentation to reveal further useful research data.

■ ■ ■ Task: Designing an observation schedule

1. Choose a small group of about four pupils.
2. Design an observation schedule containing specific points that you wish to observe. This could be linked to the research questions you devised for Chapter 5.
3. Observe the pupils for one lesson with scans every three minutes.
4. In a few sentences say what the observation has shown.
5. Present stages 1 to 4 to your research group for discussion.

■ ■ ■ Suggested further reading

Powell, G. Chambers, M. and Baxter, G. (2002) *Pathways to Classroom Observation: A Guide for Team Leaders*. Bristol: TLO.

The authors consider the use of observation as part of a team approach to school improvement. Through a number of cases they illustrate how observation can be used in creating strategies for change. The text is laid out clearly in the format of a training manual. This book will be of particular value to those involved in school development.

Simpson, M. and Tuson, J. (1995) *Using Observations in Small-Scale Research: A Beginner's Guide*. Edinburgh: Scottish Council for Research in Education (SCRE).

This is a useful introductory text on observation as a research method. It presents practical examples showing how to organize observation, record data and analyse the findings.

■ ■ ■ Chapter 10

Use of existing documents

■ ■ ■ Introduction

This chapter considers the variety of existing documentary material that provides useful data for practitioner research. This can take many forms ranging from national curriculum documents, OFSTED reports on specific schools to records of pupil attainment within a particular class. Pupil reports and schemes of work are looked at as examples. The chapter then goes on to consider the analysis of written curriculum materials used by teachers and photographic evidence analysed by pupils.

■ ■ ■ Existing written evidence

There is already much qualitative and quantitative data written about every school and place of education that can be used by the researcher, for example, OFSTED reports, national curriculum assessment data, external examination results, attendance and pupil exclusion statistics. There is also a great deal of documentation produced at all levels of the education service, for example, school prospectuses, development plans and policies on all aspects of the curriculum. There is also other written documentation that may be useful, if less readily available, such as the minutes of staff, department and governors' meetings. These sources provide valuable data about all aspects of life in different educational settings. Prior (2003) contends that such documents form a field for research in their own right.

Practitioner researchers always need to bear in mind who has been involved in producing documents and collecting this official information, the type of questions these people will have been asking and also what they would not have looked at. It is important to remain critical and to recognize the different ways in which information can be officially presented. The deconstruction of such documents and data is an important area of research in itself. For example, school performance statistics may, if taken at face value, show changes in pupil achievement over time. However it is important to question why these statistics were compiled, how they were collected, what they do or do not tell us about the performance of individual pupils. As Prior (2003: 26) counsels, 'content is not the most important feature of a document'. Similar analysis can be undertaken on the construction of written documents such as official codes of conduct and school prospectuses. Such analysis will give some indication about what is valued, at least officially, in the education system.

Reporting on pupil progress

Consider the following reports to parents of pupil progress (Figures 10.1 and 10.2). They are reports on pupils from different generations of the same family and as such they are interesting historical documents in themselves (all names have been changed). They provide useful material for research into the reporting of pupil achievement to parents, curriculum development, pupil assessment, the work of teachers, expectations of pupils' achievement and so on. They give a fascinating insight into how these things have changed (or not!) over the years and you can draw your own conclusions about the level of care and detail taken over them and what this implies about the ways in which a teacher's work has changed.

The contrast between these reports cannot fail to strike us and raises different questions depending on our views of education, reporting and so on. For instance, one parent might ask how the first report could possibly convey any meaningful information about John's progress. Another may ask whether the extensive data made available on John's nephew, Peter, nearly 40 years later, is all necessary or comprehensible to the lay person. A further contrast might be drawn between the way in which reports are used by teachers as a starting point for discussion with parents; this practice is more characteristic of the present than the past.

We can see that a whole host of research uses might be made of such documents. Written documents, whilst providing evidence in themselves, are also useful in discussion with the significant parties. For

NAME	John Hughes
DATE	Dec 1964
GROUP	1
NO. IN GROUP	8
AGE	9.11
AVERAGE AGE	10.5
ENGLISH	Very good – has a good grasp of the essentials
SPELLING	Very good
COMPOSITION	Excellent ideas and always an interesting composition
MATHEMATICS	Good, but must try harder with problems
GENERAL KNOWLEDGE	Very good – gives sensible answers
CRAFT	Good on the whole, but often careless
REMARKS	John's handwriting has improved, so his work is more easily understood. He is well able to concentrate, and gains knowledge from his extensive reading. He is very musical, and has a good sense of rhythm.

■ **Figure 10.1**

A report of a pupil in a small primary school in rural England in 1964

Peter Hughes   **Report for the School Year 2002–2003**   **Year Five**

Sessions (Half days) this year: <u>310</u>
310

Attendances: 100%   Unauthorized Absences: 0
Punctuality: Satisfactory

S.E.N._____   ☐   ☐

> Throughout this report progress in learning is shown as:
> (a) is working beyond this target
> (b) has achieved this target
> (c) working towards this target

There will be an opportunity to discuss your child's report at parents' evening in July.

ENGLISH – SPEAKING AND LISTENING	a	b	c
Talks and listens with confidence in an increasing range of contexts		√	
In discussion listens carefully, making contributions and asking questions that are responsive to others' ideas and views			√

Continued over

	a	b	c
Uses appropriately some of the features of standard English vocabulary and grammar		✓	
In discussion, shows understanding of the main points		✓	

ENGLISH – READING	a	b	c
In responding to a range of texts, shows understanding of significant ideas, themes, events and characters, beginning to use inference and education		✓	
Refers to the text when explaining views		✓	
Locates and uses ideas and information		✓	
Reads a range of texts fluently and accurately	✓		

ENGLISH – WRITING	a	b	c
Ideas are often sustained and developed in interesting ways and organized appropriately for the purpose of the reader		✓	
Is beginning to use grammatically complex sentences, extending meaning		✓	
Full stops, capital letters and questions marks are used correctly and is using punctuation within the sentence		✓	
Handwriting style is fluent, joined and legible		✓	
Writing is often organized, imaginative and clear		✓	
Spelling is usually accurate, including that of common, polysyllabic words		✓	

MATHEMATICS	a	b	c
Multiply and divide any positive integer up to 10,000 by 10 or 100 and understand the effect			✓
Order a given set of positive and negative integers		✓	
Use a decimal notation for tenths and hundredths		✓	
Round a number with one or two decimal places to the nearest integer			✓
Relate fractions to division and to their decimal representations			✓
Calculate mentally a difference such as 8006–2993		✓	
Carry out column addition and subtraction of positive integers less than 10,000		✓	
Know by heart all multiplication and division of a three-digit by a single-digit integer		✓	
Carry out long multiplication of a two-digit by a two-digit integer		✓	
Understand areas measured in square centimetres (cm²) understand and use the formula in words 'length x breadth' for the area of a rectangle		✓	
Recognize parallel and perpendicular lines, and properties of rectangles		✓	
Use all four operations to solve simple word problems involving numbers and quantities including time, explaining methods and reasoning			✓

MATHS – SHAPE, SPACE AND MEASURE	a	b	c
Makes 3-D mathematical models by linking given faces or edges and draws common 2-D shapes in different orientations on grids		✓	
Reflects simple shapes in a mirror line		✓	
Chooses and uses appropriate units and instruments, interpreting, with appropriate accuracy, numbers on a range of measuring instruments		✓	
Finds perimeters of simple shapes and finds areas by counting squares		✓	

¬ATHS – HANDLING DATA	a	b	c
⁺s discrete data and records them, using a frequency table		✓	
⁻ds and uses the mode and range to describe sets of data			✓

Continued over

Groups data, where appropriate, in equal class intervals, represents
collected data in frequency diagrams and interprets such diagrams √
Constructs and interprets simple line graphs √

SCIENCE – SCIENTIFIC ENQUIRY	a	b	c
Recognizes that scientific ideas are based on evidence		√	
In own investigative work, decides on an appropriate approach (for example, using a fair test) to answer a question		√	
Where appropriate, describes or shows, in the way the task is performed, how to vary one factor whilst keeping others the same		√	
Where appropriate, makes predictions		√	
Selects suitable equipment to use and makes a series of observations and measurements that are adequate for the task		√	
Records observations, comparisons and measurements, using tables and bar charts		√	
Begins to plot points to form simple graphs and uses these graphs to point out and interpret patterns in the data		√	
Begins to relate conclusions to these patterns and to scientific knowledge and understanding, and to communicate them with appropriate scientific language		√	

SCIENCE – MATERIALS AND THEIR PROPERTIES	a	b	c
Describes differences between the properties of different materials and explains how these differences are used to classify substances such as solids, liquids and gases		√	
Describes some methods, such as filtration and distillation, that are used to separate simple mixtures		√	
Uses scientific terms, such as evaporation or condensation, to describe changes		√	
Uses knowledge about some reversible and irreversible changes to make simple predictions about whether other changes are reversible or not		√	

INFORMATION AND COMMUNICATIONS TECHNOLOGY	a	b	c
Creates sequences of instructions to control events and understand the need to be precise when framing and sequencing instructions when using logo and turtle		√	
Understands how ICT devices with sensors can be used to monitor and measure external events such as using ecotoy and digital thermometers		√	
Explores the effects of changing the variables in an ICT		√	
Discusses their knowledge and experience of using ICT and their observations of its use outside school	√		
Assesses the use of ICT in own work and can reflect critically in order to make improvements in subsequent work	√		
Adds to, amends and combines different forms of information from a variety of sources when working with Excel	√		
Uses ICT to present information in different forms and shows awareness of the intended audience and the need for quality in their presentations, e.g. when word processing and using digital camera	√		
Compares own use of ICT with other methods and with its use outside school		√	

Continued over

	a	b	c
RELIGIOUS EDUCATION (Following Shropshire Agreed Syllabus)			
Has learnt about the significance of some number in a range of world faiths.		✓	
Has developed understanding of the Journey of life and some rites of passage.		✓	
Has begun to explore the significance of water in some world religions.		✓	
Has discussed, with sensitivity, moral issues linked to the use of the world's resources, especially water.		✓	
Developing a greater sensitivity to their own spiritual growth and acknowledging the spirituality of others.		✓	

	a	b	c
HISTORY			
Uses knowledge and understanding of aspects of the history of Victorian Britain, Ancient Greece and the wider world to describe features of past societies and to identify changes within and across periods.		✓	
Is beginning to select and combine information from different sources and is beginning to produce structured work, making appropriate use of dates and terms.		✓	
Shows how some aspects of the past have been represented and interpreted in different ways.		✓	

	a	b	c
GEOGRAPHY			
Recognizes and describes physical and human processes when studying rivers and water.		✓	
Describes how people can both improve and damage the environment and explains views about environmental change.		✓	
Uses a range of books, maps, pictures and ICT in investigations and communicates findings clearly.		✓	
Is beginning to read, understand and interpret a range of maps in different scales.		✓	

	a	b	c
ART			
Explores ideas and collects visual and other information to help develop work when using sketch books for work on landscapes.		✓	
Uses knowledge and understanding of materials and processes to communicate ideas and meanings, and makes images and artefacts, combining and organising visual and tactile qualities to suit own intentions.		✓	
Compares and comments on ideas, methods and approaches used in own and others' work, relating these to the context in which the work was made, e.g. Victorian paintings and Ancient Greek pottery.		✓	
Adapts and improves work to realize own intentions.		✓	

	a	b	c
DESIGN TECHNOLOGY			
Generates ideas by collecting and using information when studying switches and the Ironbridge.		✓	
Takes users' views into account and produces step-by-step plans.		✓	
Communicates alternative ideas using words, labelled sketches and models, showing awareness of constraints.		✓	
Works with a variety of materials and components with some accuracy, ʸing attention to quality of finish and to function when designing ᵗres.		✓	
ᵈ works with a range of tools and equipment.		✓	

Reflects on their recipes as they develop bearing in mind the way the bread will be used. √
Identified what is working well and what could be improved. √

MUSIC	a	b	c
Sings and plays for performance, from ear and simple notation, with awareness of how different parts fit together.		√	
Through listening to a variety of music explores how sounds and music reflect different moods and intentions.		√	
Can improvise rhythmic phrases within a group and can suggest improvements to their own and others' work.		√	

PHYSICAL EDUCATION	a	b	c
Links skills, techniques and ideas and applies them accurately and tactically when playing invasion games.	√		
Performances show precision, control and fluency, understands composition in dance and gymnastics.		√	
Compares and comments on skills, techniques and ideas used in own and others' work, and uses this understanding to improve performance.	√		
Explains and applies basic safety principles in preparing for exercise.	√		
Describes what effects exercise has on the body, and how it is valuable to fitness and health.	√		

P.S.H.E.	a	b	c
Is learning about themselves as a growing and changing individual with own experiences and ideas, and as a member of the community.		√	
Is becoming more mature, independent and self-confident.		√	
Is learning about the wider world and the interdependence of communities within it.		√	
Is developing a sense of social justice and moral responsibility and is beginning to understand that own choices and behaviour can affect local, national or global issues and political and social institutions.		√	
Is learning how to take part more fully in school and community activities.			√
Is learning how to make more confident and informed choices about health and environment, to take more responsibility, individually and as a group, for own learning, and to resist bullying.			√

CONSIDERATION FOR OTHERS
Always polite and considerate
Polite and considerate most of the time
Sometimes needs to be reminded of the needs of others √

PRESENTATION OF WORK
Takes a pride in work:
always √
usually
sometimes

COMMENTS

ENGLISH

Peter is a fluent reader. He has a good comprehension of the text and has developed the ability to use less obvious clues to enhance his understanding of characters and plot. He has begun to analyse how words and phrases can be used to make a text more interesting. Peter writes well and is beginning to consider the most appropriate language–style to use for different types of writing. He needs to improve focus and concentration to maintain his quality throughout a longer piece of writing. Peter has very good spelling. He has learned important skills in self-editing for spelling, punctuation, grammar and style of writing and now needs to use these regularly in his own work.

MATHEMATICS
Peter has good numeracy skills. His responses to mental arithmetic questions are generally quick and accurate. He is beginning to develop skills in applying his knowledge to simple problems by working out which numeracy method is appropriate to use in which problem. This will need continued revision to ensure the skills learned become fluent. Peter's written work is usually accurate, however he needs to develop the habit of checking his calculations to ensure the minimum of errors. Peter tells me he lacks confidence to write answers unless he is certain they are correct, this may explain the difference between his, generally competent performance in whole-class discussion and less confident written work. Let's see Peter 'Go for it!' next year – don't worry about the occasional mistake.

SCIENCE
Peter has enjoyed this year's science, he has a good understanding of the topics covered and he has a developing understanding of scientific enquiry. Peter is able to draw upon past knowledge to make predictions and to question the veracity of results. Now he needs to be more exacting in his analysis of results and to take a more active role in decision-making when conducting experiments.

GENERAL COMMENTS:
Peter has a great deal of potential. He is sufficiently intelligent to do well academically and he has the charisma of a leader. These are not mutually exclusive.
Peter has made good progress in English and he now needs to put similar effort into his Maths. I hope to see Peter responding positively to the opportunities and responsibilities he will be offered next year.
Classteacher's Signature _____ Date: 21.6.03

HEADTEACHER'S COMMENT:
Excellent attendance now let us see this matched with behaviour and motivation!! Peter you can do it!
Signature _____ Date: July 03

■ **Figure 10.2**

Report of a pupil from a primary school in a town in the West Midlands in 2002

instance, it is interesting to discuss reports with teachers who write them, parents who receive them and pupils who are written about. It stimulates thoughts on many personal aspects and memories of school life. In this way such documents may help to produce rich biographical accounts. Consider John's secondary school report of several years later (Figure 10.3). Certainly there is a 'story' to be told of his journey through primary, into secondary and eventually, if the evidence were ⸱⸱ered, into employment.

HIGH SCHOOL FOR BOYS

CONFIDENTIAL REPORT ON: John Hughes Form: 3W Date: Summer 1969
Age: 14.6   Average Age: 14.3   Times Absent: 24   Times Late: Invariably

SUBJECT	Term %	Exam %	REMARKS	
ENGLISH	63	42	Produces quite good work	BW
GEOGRAPHY	17	24	Still very poor	RP
HISTORY	52	31	Careless. Unsatisfactory. Work rarely legible	ACB
LATIN	62	31	He could have done well in this subject	A
FRENCH	62	18	He should have done better.	PJH
MATHEMATICS	44	24	Much more care is needed.	PAD
PHYSICS	63	29	His work has deteriorated badly.	KH
CHEMISTRY	55	18	He could do much better.	NJ
BIOLOGY	35	23	He has made very little effort.	CP
ART	39	57	Has relaxed in effort somewhat though examination work was fairly good.	DHW
MUSIC		61	He has ability but seems afraid to use it.	NB
WOODWORK	37	24	He tries hard but is rather slow.	BEL
RELIGIOUS EDUCATION			Works well.	PR
PHYSICAL EDUCATION			Satisfactory	LW

GENERAL REMARKS

A bad report. He seems to be cultivating a lackadaisical approach to work.

Form Master

■ **Figure 10.3**

Report of a pupil in a small town secondary state grammar school in 1969

In looking back at his father's report from the same school over 30 years previously (Figure 10.4), what is most striking is how little change had been made in the reporting format and comments of the two reports. The names of the curriculum subjects are in some cases significantly different, however.

HIGH SCHOOL FOR BOYS

Report Form   July 28th 1933
Name: L. Hughes   Form Remove

Times Absent 2   Age 12.11   No. in Form 30
Times Late 0   Average Age of Form 12.9 *Position in Form 8*

SUBJECT	NO. IN FORM	POSITION	REMARKS	
SCRIPTURE	29	5	*Good*	
ENGLISH	30	6	*Strong progress*	GB
GEOGRAPHY	30	4	*V.Good*	GWA
HISTORY	30	3	*Very Good*	FD
LATIN				
FRENCH	30	7=	*Has worked hard*	ROW
ARITHMETIC	30		*Tries hard*	JIW
ALGEBRA				
GEOMETRY	30	16=	*More effort needed*	JIW
TRIGONOMETRY				
PHYSICS	30	17	*Capable of doing better*	EJ
CHEMISTRY				
NATURE STUDY				
ART	30	12=	*Good*	RS
SINGING	30	16=	*Satisfactory*	HCMB
MANUAL WORK	30	14=	*Good*	AS
PHYSICAL EXERCISES	30	9	*Satisfactory*	AS
GAMES			*Good*	AS

CONDUCT Good   Weekly Detentions: 0 times

GENERAL CONDUCT AND PROGRESS: *L. hUGHES has made good progress on the whole and his conduct is satisfactory.*

Next Term begins on   **signed** Form Master

■ **Figure 10.4**

Report of a pupil in a small town secondary state grammar school in 1933

■ ■ ■ Teachers' lesson planning

Other documents that can inform us of school life are the lesson plans written by teachers. Here are two examples of teacher planning. The first (Figure 10.5) was a plan for two weeks' teaching written by a primary school teacher in 1951. The second (Figure 10.6) is an example used by student teachers of a week's lessons on the literacy hour in 2002. Such documents provide striking evidence of the way practice changes over time and prompt further questions to be asked concerning the whole nature of teaching and classroom life.

Teaching Plans for Infants (age 5–7)

Easter Term 1951

	Week ending 12th Jan (average 8 in class)	Week ending 19th Jan (average 8)
NUMBER	2x,3x tables. s..d table to 15d. Individual work from cards Practical shopping up to 1/-	2x, 3x, s..d tables – Number bonds of 5 Individual work from cards Shopping and weighing sand
LANGUAGE	News sheet	News sheet and weather record
ACTIVITIES	Transcription from copies Top Group : Exercises from 'Ability Exercises' Book I. Poetry – An evening prayer	Std I – Simple comprehension on picture – 'The Farmyard' → ditto
NATURE & OBSERVATION	Nature walk, and looking at a small stream Simple talk on river action, depth, undercutting and flooding	Story : Serial 'Teddy Bear's Birthday Party' Nature story with picture to show difference in animals' footprints in the snow
PHYSICAL EDUCATION	Indoors – music and movement. Short apparatus practices outdoors.	→ ditto → ditto
MUSIC	'Rag Dolls' action song Music and Movement	'Buttercups & Daisies' Music & Movement 'Rag Dolls'
HANDWORK ACTIVIITIES	Free activity Renewing some goods for the shop Painting – free expression 'Of Nature Walk'	Free activity with all available materials → ditto Some – woodwork

---

■ **Figure 10.5**

Planning by a teacher in a primary school in a rural school on the English/Welsh border

NATIONAL LITERACY STRATEGY TEACHING OBJECTIVES – WEEKLY PLANNER: PRIMARY SCHOOL

Class: 5   Yr Group (s): 5 | Term: Spring – 1st half | Week Beg: 21st Jan 02 | Teacher

	Whole-class shared reading writing	Whole-class phonics, spelling vocabulary and grammar	Guided group tasks (reading or writing)	Guided group tasks (reading or writing)	Independent group tasks	Plenary
Mon	Look at front cover illustration and title. What kind of information might they find? Use of question words in the title. Revise term explanation. P.8–9 – read the text and caption. Explanation text p.2–3 – use acetate and annotate.	Investigate and note features of impersonal style. Spellings – 10 words with suffix changing from full/ful.	ALS Group: Guided reading – Level 8.		Using a selection of non-fiction books look at contents pages of each book and identify whether the book is likely to contain explanations. Makes notes and list anything that supports their choice e.g. contents structure etc.	1 group to report back on activity. Return to page 2–3 using PCM 1. 1 large copy and A4 for pupils. What is an explanation text?
Tues	Read model text p.2–3. Discuss tone/level of formality of text. Does the author address the reader directly? Are personal opinions given? Paragraph 3 – identify verbs. Repeat verbs p.6–7	Investigate verbs of past and present tense. Junior English p.58.	Red Group: Guided reading – Level 9.		Using one of the explanations from lesson 1 ask the children to identify and list all the verbs in the present tense. Ask if verbs are used to explain how things happen or how things are. Ext: put verbs into sentences in present tense.	1 group to report back. Are the words chosen actually verbs? If so are they in the present tense? How do we know?
Wed	Read model text p.2–3. Look at connectives. Discuss how explanations are linked e.g. because, so. P.5 – read first sentence. Look at a how a complex sentence can be made into 2 shorter sentences. Repeat with para. Mammals on land.	Pronouns. Junior English p.21	Blue Group 2: Guided reading –Level 10.		Ask children to identify and list further cause and effect connectives in other explanation texts. Using PCM 2 pupils to practice combining sentences.	Add connectives children have found to the list and discuss the appropriate use of commas. Use PCM 2.
Thur	Mask captions on p.10 and 11. Read p.11 – the inner ear. Discuss with the children how they think an ear works. What helps their explanations and understandings? Ask children.	Joining sentences. Junior English p.31.	Yellow Group 2: Guided reading – Level 10.	Blue Group 1: Guided reading – Level 10.	Using prepared books with masked captions ask the children to work in pairs to examine illustrations, diagrams and photographs and write captions for them.	Ask some pupils to read out their own captions before revealing the real caption. Ensure others provide comment.
Fri	Sports Link Taster Day.				Sports Link Taster Day.	

■ **Figure 10.6**
An example of a student teacher's planning for one week of literacy hour lessons (Liverpool JMU)

What do these documents tell us or rather what questions do they prompt?

- Is the planning of 1951 so cursory as to be worthless or is the teacher so experienced that she does not need more than these minor prompts? (A journey back in time to see this planning in action would be most instructive).

- Does planning a whole week's literacy hour lessons allow sufficient flexibility for pupils to make differential progress each day?

- To what extent does each planning sheet facilitate differentiation?

- How is planning in either case related to assessment?

- What do these examples tell us about the relative autonomy of the teachers in terms of the curriculum?

- How slavishly do lessons follow teacher planning documents in practice?

■ ■ ■ Analysis of teaching texts

Thus far we have considered written documents used in educational institutions; it is also important to consider the texts that are used in the teaching process. It is these texts that make up a significant part of the curriculum that the pupils receive at school. They carry messages, sometimes intended and sometimes not, that children take with them from the classroom. It is interesting to consider the content of school texts and how they create images of what is officially important in history, geography, citizenship and so on.

In the 1980s there was much interest in the gender and racial stereotyping portrayed in the texts and reading books used in schools. As a result of having developed equal opportunities policies, schools and LEAs began to monitor the published material that was used by their pupils. Useful research tools were developed by, for example, Genderwatch (Myers, 1992), for practitioners to use. The examples in Figures 10.7 and 10.8 were tools for analysing the content of books used in the classroom.

Name of school _____

Filled in by _____ Date completed _____..

F   M   (please tick)

- Are the authors, contributors and editors, men or women? _____
- How many men and women are named in the CONTENTS list? _____
- How many men and women are in the INDEX? _____
- How many times are women mentioned in the TEXT? _____
- Do they appear as independent people or as DEPENDENTS on men (wives, etc.)?
- Are they shown in a wide range of activities or limited to STEREOTYPED ACTIVITIES (housewives, spinning, social reformers)?
- Are they described in the same way as men or is APPEARANCE emphasized?
- How many ILLUSTRATIONS include: women? _____ men? _____
- How many illustrations are there of specific women and men?_____
- Does LANGUAGE exclude stereotypical descriptions of women e.g. man, workman, farmer and wife? _____
- Does the SUBJECT MATTER, e.g. in history, emphasize and value concerns traditionally associated with men, e.g. war, diplomacy, trade, parliament, inventions, rather than concerns traditionally associated with women, e.g. family life, work, housing, local politics, living standards?

_____

■ Figure 10.7

Checklist for assessing sex bias in non-fiction books for older pupils (designed by Carol Adams, in Myers, 1992, Genderwatch)

This type of pro forma proved very useful as it could either be used as it was or could be easily modified as required. What such research provided for those schools that undertook it was data that enabled them to analyse their current literature provision. This formed the basis of staff discussion from which future policy could be developed and suitably monitored. Though the examples shown above relate to gender they could be easily adapted to capture data relating to ethnicity, religion and other socio-cultural issues. Although originally designed for analysing books, the same methodology could be employed in the assessment of other curriculum and display material used throughout the school.

Name of school..

Filled in by...................... Date completed ....

How many pictures are there of women/girls in your book? _____

How many pictures are there of men/boys in your book? _____

List the activities the people illustrated are doing

Women/girls _____

Men/boys _____

Are there differences between the types of activities women/girls are shown doing compared with those that men/boys are doing?

Explain _____

_____

■ **Figure 10.8**

Checklist for assessing sex bias in non-fiction books for younger pupils (Myers, 1992, Genderwatch! After the Education Reform Act. *Cambridge: Cambridge University Press)*

■ ■ ■ Photographs and their use in research

Traditionally, academic work and the research upon which it was based has usually been presented in written form. It may have been that this was the only appropriate manner in which to transmit such material. However if, as is said, a picture can paint a thousand words then the importance of using photographic evidence in classroom-based research must also be considered. Bartlett et al. (2001) have discussed the power of photographic evidence in depicting school organization and teaching style in nineteenth-century schools. The starkness of huge rooms with pupils in serried rows and the 'master' on a raised dais with cane in hand needs little textual elaboration.

For practitioners, photographs and video evidence can often help an explanation and can provide illustration of what has been observed by the researcher or discussed in interviews. As with all methods of data collection, the researcher will use photographic evidence as they see appropriate to the study. Whilst considering visual evidence presented in photographs, it is important to remain aware of the 'snapshot' nature of such images and how the particular content has been framed at the expense of something else.

Thus photographic evidence needs to be interpreted and there follows a study that looked at how pupils themselves analyse such images. It was carried out by Tony Pickford, who had been a geography teacher in primary schools for a number of years prior to working in initial teacher education. He was very interested in how pupils interpret photographic images. He had used pictures in his teaching over a period of years and had assumed that pupils were able to interpret images presented to them in much the same way as adults. He had come, over a period of time, to the realization that this taken-for-granted assumption was highly questionable. An account of his study follows presented as he wrote it for discussion with practising primary teachers and student teachers in the form of a study unit.

Visual Literacy & Graphicacy: A Short Study Unit for Primary Teachers and Trainees by Tony Pickford

'Visual literacy as a field of research, study, and teaching becomes increasingly important with the ever-expanding proliferation of mass media in society. As more and more information and entertainment is acquired through (images), the ability to think critically and visually about the images presented becomes a crucial skill.'

Benedict I & J
Visual Literacy Collection http://www.asu.edu/lib archives/bvlc.htm
Accessed on 26th June 2003

Graphicacy
- *Graphicacy:*   'Communication of information that cannot be conveyed by verbal or numerical means alone'
- *Visual Literacy:* 'the ability to understand and produce visual messages'

Writers, such as Mackintosh (1998) argue that the development of children's visual literacy is at least as important as development of their print literacy or numeracy skills. In a society where so much information is conveyed by visual means, the development of a critical understanding of visual information is vital. Research has shown that 'visual perception is a form of information processing which changes with age' (Mackintosh 1998) and children need to be taught to 'read' and interpret visual images.

Research by Long (1953) found that seven-year olds seem not to see a picture as a whole, but as a series of separate details. Before investigating ways in which children might be encouraged to develop their graphicacy skills, I decided to see if the conclusions of this fifty-year old research might still be valid.

Research

I asked the teacher of a Year 1 class in an urban primary school to present individual children with two images: the first chosen because of its level of detail and the second because it is similar to many others found in primary geography photo-packs about distant localities. The teacher asked the simple question: 'What does this picture show?' and taped the children's spontaneous responses. I asked the teacher to help children to name unfamiliar objects in the images, but to give no other help.

Details in Images

The Y1 (six year old) children responded to the question, 'What does this picture show?' by reciting lists of the details they could see in each picture.

Child A responded to the first picture, as follows:

'*inaudible* ... ... and people ... and houses ... and trees ... and birdies'

Child B said: 'soldiers ... horses ... houses ... waters(?) ... baddies'

Child C saw 'penguins ... trees'

Child A responded to the second image, as follows: 'Grass ... oranges and apples ... grapes ... *(with help)* aubergines ... vegetables'

Child D saw only the scales in Image 2 and Child B could only identify 'sausages'.

Most adults presented with these images tend to give each picture a title or label which encompasses the content of the picture. Image 1 is often described as 'A snow Scene' or 'Hunters'. Image 2 may be labelled as 'A market stall'. Unlike young children, adults try to take in the whole picture and give it a title.

This evidence suggests that young children may perceive images in a different way from adults – they take in the details of a picture, often without reference to the relevance or relative importance of the details to the whole image. Or perhaps, they articulate the process which adults carry out 'in their heads', prior to giving a title.

If so, then the children in this small-scale research did not go on to draw the conclusion (or picture title) that adults tend to.

The two images are:
Image 1: 'Hunters in the Snow', a painting by Breughel
Image 2: A photograph of a stall-holder and his stall in a market in Kabul, Afghanistan

Implications
Younger children (Reception class – Year 2) may see pictures as a series of separate details

- They notice foreground and large background objects, but tend to ignore the middle ground;
- 'Year 2 children pick on lots of detail, especially foreground detail, including things that are relatively unimportant to the understanding of the photograph including peripheral objects, but not necessarily the main essence of the picture' (Stott 1994);
- They tend not to take in the 'whole picture' – or, at least, if they do, they do not verbalize their conclusions;
- In the classroom, they should be presented with lively, 'peopled' pictures with lots of detail and be encouraged to give a title to an image.

Older children (KS2 onwards)
- Begin to identify main points of a picture
- Begin to generalize and take in the 'whole picture'

For a more detailed short outline of research in this area, please read Mackintosh M (1998) Learning from Photographs in Scoffham S (Ed.) Primary Sources: Research Findings in Primary Geography Geographical Association, Sheffield

Teaching Graphicacy
The teaching of graphicacy remains vitally important, even with older children, in that many visual conventions which adults take for granted will still need to be explicitly taught if children are to make sense of the range of visual images we expect them to use, especially

in classroom contexts. Aldrich & Shepherd (2000) carried out a survey of books used in the teaching of primary science and found that many used visual images which could be confusing or misleading to children, if they were not explained and/or decoded by the teacher.

We have made very few amendments to how Tony actually presented his research. What makes this a useful example of practitioner research is in illustrating how he has developed his professional interest in the area of visual literacy. His reading helped him to refine his ideas and in the light of it he was able to design his own small-scale research project. This has now moved further as he is extending the research to look at other images. His research influences his teaching with children in school and in discussion with other practising teachers and trainee teachers. Likewise, what he learns from his teaching is also reflected in how his research interest continues to develop.

■ ■ ■ Advantages of using extant documents

1. They help provide official versions of how different education institutions, curricula and assessment operate at a particular point in time.
2. They demonstrate changes over time.
3. They often generate further questioning by the researcher.
4. They are a useful stimulant for further discussion by those involved.
5. They provide recorded data that may have been forgotten or not known by research participants.

■ ■ ■ Disadvantages of using extant documents

1. Written accounts may not be an accurate reflection of events as they reflect the view or wishes of the compilers and may have been rendered politically correct.
2. The documents alone do not show how they were interpreted and

used by the researcher so triangulation via other data sources beyond the documents themselves is advisable.

■ ■ ■ Conclusion

All documentary material, whatever its source, be it government, publisher, school management team, teachers or even pupils themselves, can provide an insight into life in educational institutions. Such material can enhance or be enhanced by data gathered via various other research methods such as interviews, observation and questionnaires. Documentation may provide a stimulus for interview or observation or it may provide useful contextual or explanatory data for something a researcher has found through questionnaires, observations, and so on. In our final look at possible research methods, we consider in Chapter 11 the use of reflective biographies and logs.

■ ■ ■ Task: Identifying and analysing existing documentation

1.   Make a list of documents that have been written by staff at your school that could be used to illustrate school life.

2.   Choose a sample of these documents. What do these tell you about your school? Analyse them in terms of the following headings: school aims, the curriculum, teaching and learning, relationships.

■ ■ ■ Suggested further reading

Prior, L. (2003) *Using Documents in Social Research.* London: Sage.

The forms, compilation and social significance of documents are discussed and the author considers the role of such documents in research. Though not specifically written for education researchers, the text is relevant for users across a range of subject areas.

■ ■ ■ Chapter 11

Research biographies and logs

■ ■ ■ Introduction

This chapter looks at biographical accounts that can supply data for the research or form part of the analysis. Research diaries and logs are also examined as a means of collecting data that monitors a process over time.

■ ■ ■ What is biography?

Biographies are written accounts of a person's life or a certain aspect of it. The account may be written by the subject themselves or a biographer who, when the biography is for a research project, is likely to be the researcher. Roberts (2002) suggests that biographical research subsumes various related approaches to the study of individuals. Writing a biography is a useful way of bringing different types of data together into a coherent account in order to explain something about a person. The writing of the biography itself is actually part of the analysis. As the extract from Usher (1995) discussing *auto*biography as a research method explains,

> Autobiography (or telling the story of the self) has achieved considerable prominence in pedagogy and educational research. It appears ideally suited to revealing experience-based learning and in tracking the development of the self as learner … The autobiographical subject makes himself … an object of examination … Autobiography then becomes a process of writing the self, of telling the story of the self through a written text and of writing the text through a culturally encoded meta-story … This central assumption that a life 'as it really is' can be captured and represented in a text has been increasingly questioned. It is now becoming accepted that an

autobiography is not immediately referential of a life but is instead a work of artifice or fabrication that involves reconstructing the self through writing the self. Changing and shifting identity is 'fixed' and anchored by the act of writing. In the poststructuralist story the emphasis is on writing, the production of text. Life itself is conceived as a social text, a fictional narrative production. (1995: 1).

To some extent the way in which an autobiographical account is a fictional reconstruction rather than a life itself also applies to biographical accounts written of others by researchers. The researcher reconstructs what has been observed or learned about the participant by selecting particular elements, emphasizing certain actions, inferring meaning or motive and, as such, is analysing the data as it unfolds. Evans et al. (2000: 418) report how an action research group of teachers who came together to improve their practice approached their work by writing a story about a pressing professional concern. To illustrate the use of biography as a means of synthesizing and presenting data that has been collected using several research methods, we have extracted from a larger study than many of those previously used in this book (see case study). This researcher, who worked in teacher education, had a long-standing interest in the teaching of the more able pupil from when she used to work in primary school as a class teacher. This ultimately led to her carrying out PhD research into the teaching of more able children in Key Stage 2.

Case study

Title:
An exploration into how effective upper Key Stage 2 teachers manage to intervene with more able children in the classroom setting.
This study explored how eight teachers, who had been identified from various sources as being effective, intervened in the teaching of more able children in their classes.

Methodology:
Classroom observation was the main form of data collection and there was a combination of techniques used.

■ Audio recordings of teacher talk which were transcribed for analysis.

- Field notes using:

  Lesson scripts – systematic observation and recording every two minutes of the teacher and two able children.

  Lesson protocols – non-systematic observation and recording of what the teacher and the more able children were doing and saying during a classroom episode.

Further data was collected from:

- Video recordings of selected lessons to provide contextual information.

- The product of children's work.

- Digital photographs of classroom activity, organisation and management.

- Documentation analysis (LEA policy on more able children, school policies and teacher planning notes).

- Informal interviews/discussions with the teacher.

- Semi-structured interviews with the headteachers and teachers.

The practitioner researcher outlined three stages of analysis:

Stage 1. Focusing on what teachers do (classroom observation). This involved building up a broad description of how the teachers involved themselves with the learning of the more able children.

Stage 2. Focusing on what headteachers and teachers say (interviews). This involved drawing on what the headteachers said about the identified teacher: their teaching experience, current position and responsibilities. Whole-school issues regarding the identification of and provision for the more able within their schools were also highlighted. Attention was paid, in the semi-structured teacher interview, to the teacher's philosophy on teaching and learning generally and specifically with the more able, and to their conception of ability.

Stage 3. The telling of each teacher's story. From all of the data gathered a series of 'stories' were constructed, describing in detail the way in which the teacher supports the learning.

(By Linda Rush)

In order to give a flavour of the biographies used in this study, two examples of 'teacher stories' are included. However, for the purposes of this book they have been selected from and adapted rather than reproduced in full.

■ ■ ■ Teacher story C: Sam

Teaching experience, current position and responsibilities

At the time of this study Sam had been teaching for eight years but was relatively new to his present school which he joined as a teaching deputy two and half terms previously. Prior to this Sam had worked in two schools, one of which was open plan. Very recently Sam had supported his headteacher and school staff through an OFSTED inspection. In the OFSTED report Sam's 'good support of the headteacher' and his 'ability to combine full teaching and managerial roles successfully' was highlighted. The quality of Sam's teaching was also referred to:

> The majority of the very good [and excellent] lessons occur in the top years of Key stage 2. These lessons have good pace, questioning is precise and the teacher makes sure that the main teaching points of the lesson are effectively achieved and understood. Praise and encouragement are used well to keep pupils motivated and interested. Classroom management is of a high standard and the relationships between teacher and pupils is good. (OFSTED Report, 1997/98)

Sam's headteacher described him as being:

> a naturally good teacher. He has this charisma in dealing with children. They are interested in him and the things that he has to teach them. He works extremely hard. He organizes himself well. He's very busy but always has time for anything extra that's needed. He sets very high standards ... He's a sociable person ... His particular strengths, as he sees them, are probably science, design and tech-

nology and physical education. But he's also a very good maths and English teacher. His one weakness, which he would admit, is music. I don't think he's particularly [strong in] creative subjects such as art. But at the same time he's well organized to teach the creative side and manages to do so, simply because of hard work rather than natural talent ...

However, whilst the OFSTED report had been positive about Sam's teaching and the quality of learning he promoted, it also reported concerns about the school's overall effectiveness. Whole-school planning was in its early stages and very little of the perceived school philosophy on the support of learning (classroom organization and management, assessment, behaviour management) was formally documented. Consequently, practice was inconsistent and a lack of continuity and progression prevailed in terms of the children's learning.

The researcher has begun her teacher's story effectively by providing a useful biopic of Sam, the context in which he works, current teaching and learning issues facing the school and two assessments of Sam's teaching skills. In this way we are cued in to consider what the researcher observed and learned about Sam's teaching approach and in particular his methods of working with more able pupils.

Level(s) of teacher interaction

Out of 174 minutes, teaching observed (maths, history and English) Sam spent approximately 45 per cent (80 minutes) of his time interacting with his children at whole-class level and 48 per cent (84 minutes) with groups (usually pairs) of children, less so individuals. Evidence of non-interactive teaching was limited – approximately 7 per cent (10 minutes). A negligible amount of time was spent by Sam on housekeeping issues to do with management of resources, groupings and activities, or maintaining children on task. Actual time spent with his more able at group and/or individual level amounted to approximately 10 per cent (18 minutes).

The researcher makes no reference here to time spent by Sam on behavioural matters – she clearly made a decision based on her view of what was important not to explore this issue. She will have legitimated this decision when describing and explaining her research questions. It is important, however, that readers of her research note this as, in a different context, another researcher may have considered teacher time spent responding to behavioural issues as a more prominent factor.

Nature of interaction

Whilst Sam initiated the focus of learning and designed the tasks to facilitate that learning, there was much that he did to promote equability of status between him as teacher and the children as learners. For example, in all the lessons observed a warm and friendly climate for learning prevailed in which children's efforts were regularly praised and contributions valued. Sam had a particularly good sense of humour and his use of language was inclusive:

> ... you are coming up with far too many that I didn't want you to but I will put them down anyway ... (6–8 minutes).
> ... I have put 'show your working out'. This is so important because some of you have got some good ideas about what you want to do ... (12–14 minutes).
> ... it's quite an interesting thing that you are doing ... there is nothing wrong in doing that, like I said, as long as you explain what you are doing ... (32–34 minutes).
> (Transcript of mathematics lesson)

> ... you will recall ... we were looking ... I think we have done pretty well there actually (0–2 minutes).
> ... we want to focus in on what life must have been like for those sailors ... How could we do that? How could I find out ... ? Hayley, what do you think? ... That's an interesting point ... (2–4 minutes).
> ... what were you going to say Alison? ... We are going down a different place here but it is quite interesting ... (4–6 minutes).
> (Transcript of history lesson)

Data recorded on lesson scripts indicate that the children were listening as respondents rather than passively: 'hands up to answer or voluntary interjection'. There was also plenty of discussion observed between peers – sharing and confirming thoughts before addressing the teacher at whole-class level. At the start of each lesson Sam spent time questioning the children carefully, encouraging them to explain their thought processes and explain their arguments. Questioning at this stage was not used to teach new knowledge, but to help pupils to know and use what they already have (Nisbet, 1990, cited in Freeman, 1998: 23–4).

The researcher is analysing Sam's teaching style by selecting from the lesson transcripts to enhance certain features. She is also relating her analysis to previous research literature. These are elements of good practice in writing up a study but again the researcher must be alert to the power she is able to exert over what she chooses to include/exclude and which literature she chooses to cite.

   There follow in the study several detailed examples of teacher talk and pupil talk in a number of observed lessons. Illustrations of board work, photographs of pupils talking with the teacher as part of the work are also included to aid the 'teacher story'. We now move towards the end of the account.

Planning of interaction

Apart from the English lesson there was no evidence of short-term planning. However, Sam's medium-term planning was reasonably detailed, identifying learning outcomes, activities, organization, assessment priorities, resources and notes for further planning. Specific reference to interaction was not evident, but implied through the learning outcomes and assessment opportunities highlighted. This implied interaction was certainly borne out in the lessons observed.

It is worth considering whether a different research methodology would have revealed this 'implied interaction'. Is Linda Rush overinterpreting from her evidence by attributing to Sam the indirect planning of interaction? Or does the mix of research tools – observation, access to teacher planning notes, teacher interviews – render Linda able to reach such conclusions legitimately?

Provision for the more able

Whilst interaction with the more able was limited at group and individual level, the more able did interact with Sam directly during whole-class interactions and these interactions were often initiated by the more able, not Sam. Apart from maths, science and English where the children were (broadly speaking) ability grouped, Sam preferred to group his children socially across the curriculum.

Even within the core subjects overt labelling of groups was not strong. With this emphasis on the social mix rather than the intellectual Sam usually changed the layout of the room on a termly basis so that relationships between children could be shared over the course of an academic year. He preferred to differentiate by outcome and support rather than by task. How well this was done was reliant on his very good knowledge of the children, and an excellent expertise of the subject being taught. Observed practice fitted with Sam's notion of effective teaching:

> it is important that you know your children ... know what level they are working at. That's number one I would think. You have got to have a very good knowledge of the subject that you are teaching, whatever that subject may be, certainly be several steps ahead of the children. You need to have confidence in your knowledge of the subject to be able to teach that properly ... Relationships with the children ... if you want the best out of them you have to know how to motivate them ... Planning I guess [is very important too], having formulated a plan for whatever the subject may be, knowing where that is going to go, where it is going to take you forward. What the next step will be along the road, if you like ... (Teacher interview)

Sam went on to say that he thought the overriding purposes of teaching the more able were to 'get the best out of them, thinking constantly about whether you are challenging them and whether they are working to their full potential' (Teacher interview). In the maths lesson different tasks (covering the same theme) were constructed to take into account a range of abilities. In the English and history lesson the same task was given to all children and accompanied by a prompt sheet which was usually discussed at whole-class level.

Here although the researcher steers clear of making direct judgments about the efficacy of Sam's approach with the more able, we can detect her views from such phrases as 'overt labelling of groups was not strong', ' how well this was done was reliant on his very good knowledge of the children and an excellent expertise of the subject being taught'. A different researcher may have had a bias towards differentiation by task and consequently have described Sam's approach to the more able less positively.

■ ■ ■ Teacher story E: Anna

It is interesting to consider briefly another of Linda's teacher stories, that of Anna, a deputy head in a primary school who taught a Year 6 class. Linda used the same organizing principles that she had in Sam's story, providing details on teaching experience, current position and responsibility, moving on to describe the fruits of her data gathering through the same headings of 'levels of teacher interaction', 'nature of interaction' and so on. We can see from the following extracts how interested Linda became in the pedagogic strategies that Anna used and the extent to which the teacher story became interwoven with Linda's analysis of the teaching and learning experience Anna was engaged with.

Anna believed that effective teaching required the teacher to be very clear about the learning objectives and to be very organized: 'You've got to know what you want out of them [children] and how you want them to go about doing it … but you also need to allow the very able child to do things differently to what you thought. You've got to be flexible.' Having reviewed prior learning and established present levels of knowledge and understanding, learning was consolidated and/or applied via tasks set at whole-class level. For the three lessons reported on, differentiation was by outcome in that the same task was set for everyone in mixed ability groupings (science) or the same tasks were to be worked through by everyone over a short period of time (mathematics and English). Anna acknowledged that the tasks set for mathematics were 'fairly light hearted' but felt that this was appropriate since the children had been in receipt of sustained testing during the previous week (SATs). The maths homework however was more challenging, highlighting Anna's concern for real understanding:

> Some of you, I noticed last week had a problem in the SATs with problem-solving so for homework I'm giving you some problems. The strategy used is important. I am going to ask you to do only six on the sheet ... you have to read it, you can use any strategy you want ... on the back, I don't just want the answer because I'm going to ask you tomorrow to explain how you did it. They are not difficult but I want you to explain. (Lesson protocol and video, 18 May 1998, 50–60 minutes).

The content of the science lesson conformed to the children's present experiences and, as such, had the potential to promote meaningful learning. There was also an expectation on behalf of Anna for the children to take a dual role in the management of learning.

With the exception of the science lesson, tasks set at whole-class level were completed by the children individually, even though they were sat in ability groups. Whilst there was some discussion at group level during the maths and English lessons, this tended to be limited. Anna's interaction at small group and individual level during all lessons observed was primarily a combination of monitoring and checking and consolidating conceptual framework for learning. With the exception of the guided reading group in English, support of groups in task, where a teacher listens in and adds to the children's accounts of thinking was limited.

During the teacher interview Anna was explicit about the limitations of closed procedure as an approach 'It's as it is, it's closed'. Rather than closed procedure she preferred 'something that delves into their [children's] understanding'. With Year 6 Anna liked to get them to write their own notes: 'One way I get them to do it is that we talk about it and we structure it on the board and I put phrases up which they give me and they basically have to interlink the phrases.' She went on to explain how, depending on the ability of the individual child, a differing level of detail would be required. She then went on to explain another form of note writing which she deployed when using a video to facilitate learning:

> I get them to write notes under a grid ... split it up into [sections] – plot, character, setting. I'll actually stop the video at certain points and they write down certain points or they'll have been certain questions about it. And they do this as they go through and they build this into their own notes, and I might, say, with the good ones, not

get them to answer questions but to write as a flow, as a set of notes or narratives.

Anna also felt that oral starts (numerically or verbally) were useful as a warm-up to sessions: 'I think it is really useful for them because it gets them thinking ... if you go straight into something it's dead often and they're not switched on.' Anna explained that she had long deployed the idea of a warm-up to a teaching session and that her practice had not been influenced by the literacy or numeracy hour: 'I've always done that because it works.' She described how, often when starting a new topic, she would get the children to write in the back of their books as much as they know about the particular topic being explored: 'The light one was really good, we got a fantastic set of notes out of that ... we really covered a fantastic amount of work in one session by their own contributions and they were pooling their own knowledge and sparking off one another.' Finally, Anna also believed that homework was a very useful way of fostering deeper learning: 'Homework can be used to either start a topic or finish a topic, extend the work ... I think homework is a very useful tool.'

The children usually sat in ability groups even though collaborative/co-operative group work was limited. Differentiation was primarily by outcome but during the interview Anna also mentioned that she differentiated by task. She explained, however, that to differentiate by task all the time was difficult: 'To be quite honest you can't always differentiate by task – you'd be run ragged'. More importantly for Anna was teacher expectation: 'setting your stall out and having different expectations and making it quite explicit to the groups of children'. Anna felt that a well-resourced classroom was essential for the more able child: 'preferably [one with] more computers because I think they should have more access to their own learning in that sense. Ideally a fantastic number of books, as many as possible'. She also believed that the more able children be given the opportunity to manage their own environment, to set a climate in which they are involved: 'It's that enabling to me, enabling that bright child to manage their own learning and to teach them to organize themselves.' She thought that they would prefer a teacher who:

is fairly able themselves ... If you've got somebody who isn't, I think they are very frightened of more able children ... They don't let the child go off at a tangent, if necessary ... So it has to be somebody who is academically able and very flexible or somebody who has the confidence to say 'I don't know, let's find out'. Confidence is a big thing. If you haven't got this you won't succeed with an able child because they will undermine you, and they will suss that straight away.

She went on to say that she believed that a teacher of the more able needed to be 'confident, flexible and able'. In terms of ability she believed that it helped if the teacher was academically bright:

you've got to be aware of where you're heading off to. Ideally someone with a broad base of knowledge themselves and interests, someone who could talk to them [more able] at their own level and extend them or push them on. Someone [who is] not afraid to do secondary work with them, if that's what it takes.

Rather than be strait-jacketed by the Year 6 National Curriculum Anna believed that: 'there's no harm in pushing them that bit further and extending their horizons – taking a lateral approach'. Finally, she stated that the overriding purposes of teaching the more able was to do with

Giving them a thirst for knowledge, a thirst for extending their own learning because I honestly think that a lot of more able children get a very raw deal … Always got to deal with both ends of the spectrum [ability wise] … More able children need to be kept motivated … we should be teaching them to really use their brains.

Anna said that, in part, she draws on her own experience of being a more able child in school and her son's experience.

■ ■ ■ The value of teacher stories

These 'teacher stories' show how the researcher put together and used data from several sources, such as OFSTED reports, interviews with the teachers and their headteacher, photographs showing pupils and teachers working and transcripts of lesson observations, to describe how the teachers mediated in the learning of their pupils and in particular the more able. Having constructed the stories of the different teachers, the researcher went on to compare their mediation techniques using a model of pedagogy that she adapted from previous research. In this way she was able to extrapolate from highly specific classroom based research to a theoretical model found in the literature.

As in other highly participative research forms, it is important that the researcher shares the final story with the teacher whom it portrays and that they discuss it together. This helps to maintain the researcher's accountability to the subjects of the research and is also an essential part in ensuring the validity of the study. It is always important to remember that, whilst providing very interesting, accessible and relatable accounts of how teachers work, teacher stories and biographies such as these, have been constructed on the basis of how the writer interprets the evidence.

The use of biographical accounts constructed by the teachers and pupils who themselves make up the research population is also a useful means of generating data. These accounts may be about their whole career, or their daily lives or some specific event. Some researchers ask respondents to write fictional accounts of their work or aspects of their lives based upon real-life examples (see Clough, 2002). This encourages them to reflect upon their experiences without having to disclose particular details. These narratives can then be used in discussion with the respondents. Other researchers use the device because they feel it leads them to a deeper understanding of the issue or data. Waterland, a head-teacher researching the experiences of children, parents and staff at the beginning of a school year, chose to re-create the product of three months of observation as a fictional account because 'it is only by constructing the world the child experiences within our own imaginations that we can make the world better' (2001: 138). Chapman (1999) explains that such personal narrative as a research device is congruent with a shift away from positivism toward interpretivism, where meaning has become a central focus. She reminds us that:

> there is nothing new about storying; the human need to make meaning of life's events, traumas and crises, as well as to (re)arrange the vagaries of everyday chaos into a narrative that structures unpredictability and tames uncertainty is ancient. We tell our lives, daily, in a repetition of stories, beginning and ending, rewriting and reforming ourselves ... Oral cultures, written cultures, machine cultures, electronic cultures – the common thread is the self-story. (1999: 2)

■ ■ ■ Research diaries and logs

Another way of creating written accounts that can monitor changes over time, and also record people's feelings and reactions to them, is to keep research diaries. They are different from a biography in that they are an ongoing account rather than a description that is put together later. These can be written by teachers, pupils, researchers or anyone else concerned with a particular research project. Mutually agreed headings can be used that reflect the research focus and can act as prompts for the writer. If they are written at what are agreed as appropriate intervals of perhaps every day or week or month, these diaries can provide interesting accounts of developments or even daily life as it happens. There are many examples of the use of diaries, which in shortened form are often referred to as logs, currently being developed in education. For example, pupils fill out progress logs with guidance from form tutors and class teachers, and teachers may have professional development logs that are annually updated.

The research of Clandinin and Connelly (1994) encouraged students to use life stories to reflect on their experiences as learners, teachers or administrators. Figures 11.1 and 11.2 are logs written by student teachers during their training. They are taken from examples collected by Malcolm Dixon in the School of Education, Liverpool John Moores University, and used in discussion with current students. These logs show differing amounts of factual description or reflection by the authors depending upon the particular requirements. As the student teachers progress through their training they are requested to research their own practice using the DfES standards for the award of qualified teacher status (QTS) as the criteria for their observations and judgements. Such logs might be presented as part of a trainee teacher's evidence for a school-based research task or as evidence of their growing professional competence. Teacher training tutors have also used cross-sections of such evidence to exemplify features of the 'training journey' within broader research into teacher education and training. Drever and Cope (1999), for instance, found that elements of theory taught on an initial teacher education (ITE) course could be detected within student teacher narratives, albeit somewhat subliminally!

Name: Date: 15.4.02 – 19.4.02

This week I have discovered how difficult not only differentiation within the classroom is (12 SEN children in the class), but also that spending quality time with each group appears to be impossible! During this week I feel I have not moved past the low attainers, therefore the average/high attainers have been neglected. This means that the children are being held back, therefore I need to devise a system to ensure *all* children have equal quality time spent with them. Due to this I aim to focus on one group each day.

A positive feature I have noticed that appears to be beneficial to the children is the introduction of a vocabulary/spelling book. At the beginning of each lesson I have asked the children to write two definitions of specialist vocabulary pertaining to the lesson. This way the children can refer to the definitions throughout the lesson, which not only saves time on explanations, but also reinforces the meanings of words. Coupled with this, since the children can bring the book to me for spellings, it does not detract my attention from the task I am engaged in with other children from the group.

After reflecting upon this week's teaching I feel it is important to devise another strategy to assist the children with interpretation of words. Therefore it is my intention to produce a word bank that can be placed in the middle of the table during lessons. This will need to be differentiated so as the low attainers do not have difficulty with reading the words in the bank.

Another issue that needs attention is differentiating work amongst the low attainers. Louise and James are very low attainers and cannot keep up with the other children on their table. This means additional resources will need to be devised for these two children.

■ **Figure 11.1**
Student teacher reflective log

Name: Week Ending: 1st February 2002
1. **Significant progress made in relation to the standards for QTS**
This week I have managed to teach all of the numeracy lessons as well as two science lessons and one physical education lesson. I have also taken individual groups from literacy lessons to the computer suite to develop their ICT skills in this subject area. I have also observed and worked with a science specialist on a variety of activities aimed at developing their skills in fair testing and recording results.

2. **Areas in need of further work/development in relation to the standards for QTS**
I need to continue completing my pupil progress records as well as making some progress on my school based activities. I am nearly up to date on my planning but I still need to catch up on some of my lesson evaluations. I also need to start gathering appropriate school documentation to add to my school file, which is now taking shape.
Mentor comment: The planning is very important, the amount of time you are taking on this proving to be very successful.

> 3. **Personal view of points for action next week**
> * Complete planning literacy, science and PE lessons
> * Make more progress recording and reporting on pupils' work
> * Plan for time to complete some school based activities
> * Catch up on my lesson evaluations
>
> **Mentor comment:** Just try to pace yourself.
>
> 4. **Other points**
> I now feel that I have really settled into this teaching practice. I have developed some good relationships with the pupils in both of the classes that I teach and I am really enjoying my teaching. I have a good relationship with the teachers and several have given me some good advice and support on my planning and other areas of teaching. I think that I have gained the trust and respect of the children and this has become a big help to my teaching. All aspects are going very well.
>
> **Mentor comment:** Fully agree, you look like part of the furniture – very comfortable and at home in the classroom.

■ **Figure 11.2**

Student teacher weekly self-monitoring form

Logs and diaries can provide fascinating research data which, although of a biographical nature, can enlighten educational communities in a broader sense. Although it is not possible to generalize from one person's experience it is legitimate to use this evidence to establish some aspects for further investigation. For instance an NQT and his or her mentor may keep independent weekly logs of their respective experiences in working together. It may emerge from these that there are misconceptions or different conceptions about the role of the mentor in the NQT's development. In addition to these two individuals working through these issues together, it would also be possible for the research to be broadened to other pairs to explore issues of role perception within mentoring.

■ ■ ■ Conclusion

The use of biography, logs and the fictionalizing of accumulated individual accounts is a useful way of describing and analysing processes and experiences within education. Increasingly researchers are using this method; see, for instance, Miller and West (2003) whose work has focused on auto/biographical approaches to research on adult learning and on processes of learning from experience, or Chapman (1999) who contends that educators engage so routinely in 'the discursive practices that fix educational subjects', such as grading, evaluating and assessing, that they are unnoticed as a form of 'storying'.

> Those of us in education know this, of course. Education is but one facet of the bureaucratic machine that writes us all – and in which we write or story ourselves, willingly or not; we fill in those forms, daily, weekly, monthly, yearly, as if our very lives depend upon them, as they do (1999: 2).

■ ■ ■ Task: Writing a research log

1. Identify an aspect of classroom life that you would like to monitor. This may be something in your classroom organization that you have recently changed or introduced such as homework diaries, a new system of class monitors or an express literacy or numeracy group. It may be a particular aspect of your teaching, such as the use of an interactive whiteboard or the incorporation of drama activities into lessons. It may be pupil focused such as the behaviour of particular pupils or the quality of their written work.

2. At the beginning of a new exercise book list what you consider to be the key factors about the particular focus chosen.

3. In the exercise book write between a paragraph and half a page at a set time every day on what has happened in relation to your chosen focus since the previous entry. Be sure to address the key factors. You may wish to use these key factors as subheadings. Ensure that the account for each day is clearly labelled with the date and time.

4. After two weeks summarize the contents of the log. Be sure to address the key factors and to say what changes, if any, have taken place.

5. Report on how you designed the log and findings to your research group.

■ ■ ■ **Suggested further reading**

Roberts, B. (2002) *Biographical Research*. Buckingham: Open University Press.

A range of data collection approaches that come under the heading of biography are discussed here. Methodologies are outlined that practitioner researchers will find useful but may not have previously considered such as oral history and narrative analysis.

■ ■ ■ Chapter 12

The way forward for practitioner research

■ ■ ■ Introduction

This concluding chapter reconsiders the significant contribution of practitioner research to the professional development of teachers. It goes on to make certain key observations concerning the development of research skills.

■ ■ ■ The changing nature of teacher professionalism

At the beginning of this book we considered the nature of teacher professionalism and how this is open to varying interpretations. We also looked at how the work of teachers has changed over the last 50 years and particularly since the 1970s. It can be argued that teachers are no longer encouraged to take a wider perspective on their work; years of criticism and central control have encouraged a culture of the restricted professional. When considering the role of teachers, however, there is a tension between, on the one hand, the educationalists' calls for autonomy and, on the other, the need for accountability to parents, pupils and the state. Politicians and the media have played an increasingly strident role in communicating this latter accountability to the profession and public at large.

This dual accountability leads Whitty (2002) to consider a possible future evolution towards a more 'democratic professionalism'. This implies some acceptance of the professional expertise of teachers along with a recognition that other groups share a stake in democratic decision-making in education. From the conception of a more democratic professionalism should emerge a teaching force that will reflect upon all aspects of education in a search for a deeper understanding of the learning process. As the policy context continues to change with, for instance, a re-emphasizing of creativity in the curriculum and a relaxing of attitudes towards pupil testing, practitioner research will play an increasingly important role in this search.

■ ■ ■ The role of research in professional development

Researching can be seen as an important part of the learning process so teachers who engage in research can be said to be intellectually curious. The extent to which teachers have been encouraged to be research inquisitive has, as we have seen, varied greatly over time. In the 1960s and early 1970s there was encouragement to be innovative in education. The political climate changed in the second half of the 1970s and the 1980s, and it was felt that this 'experimentation' had gone too far. There was a period of greater control exercised over the curriculum and the work of teachers. This greater accountability and the pressures to teach to set 'outcomes,' measured in terms of pupil achievement in national tests, discouraged teacher initiative and self-reflection.

From the mid-1990s there have been further developments in the professional image of teachers. There is now, once again, a desire to make teaching an 'evidence-based' profession. This involves teachers not only using evidence provided by others but becoming involved in research themselves. However, the message is very mixed. Funding to support practitioner researchers, has tended to privilege a narrow focus on methods of teaching and their effects. The promotion of practitioner research by government agencies, such as the DfES and the TTA, seems to be based upon a particular view of education linked to a positivist research perspective.

It has always been the case that teachers pursue, to varying degrees, their own professional learning and research by, for instance, attending in-service courses or studying for masters degrees. Until recently, however, this was largely left to teachers and schools to identify and fund. The current promotion of practitioner research at national policy level and any funding associated with this is therefore to be welcomed as developing a corpus of teacher researchers. Whilst many of these practitioner researchers become disenchanted with a narrow view of research, their growing research experience enables them to grapple more confidently with the complex nature of education as a contested process. We have seen in Chapter 4 that many of the practitioner researchers developed both their research skills as well as a deeper understanding of the nature of learning, teaching and the educational process. Most were inspired to look beyond and behind their initial lines of inquiry. If this is characteristic of practitioner researchers elsewhere, and we contend that it possibly is, then the practitioner research movement has the potential to engender more extended teacher professionalism amongst practitioners with the wider educational benefits that will accrue from this.

Zeichner (2003) has conducted a review of the impact of teacher research projects in the USA and, while he does not claim this to be comprehensive, the findings are encouraging. In particular, he noted the strength of teacher research groups, citing one in Massachusetts where there was

> evidence of teachers questioning their assumptions about themselves and their students and of developing new perspectives toward their practices and students. This broadening of perspective is associated with changes in the professional identities of teachers as they gain the ability to articulate more clearly their ideas about teaching and learning. (2003: 314).

Whilst conducting research was undoubtedly time-consuming and could be frustrating, projects generally led to teachers having greater confidence to influence their circumstances and control their work; looking at their teaching more analytically; taking a more learner-centred focus; and to improvements in pupil attitudes, involvement, behaviour and learning.

■ ■ ■ Research skills development

We have seen how in order for teachers to assume the role of researchers as a normal part of their professional identity they need to develop an understanding of the research process. Some of the key issues to note are that:

- There are many research methods that can be used to collect data. Even within particular method types there is enormous variation. Researchers can be inventive, not simply staying with questionnaires, surveys or formal observation. The researcher may use or adapt an existing research instrument. In many cases the researcher designs his or her own instrument.

- Researchers make decisions concerning the methodology to be used in the light of the type of data they require which is itself dependent on the purposes of the research.

- Practical constraints such as time, costs and the nature of the respondent group will be significant factors to be taken into account when designing the research. Fitness for purpose is the key criterion for deciding upon and designing a research method.

- The data collected will be a reflection of the decisions made by and the skills of the researcher.

- Researchers aim to be as rigorous as possible but inevitably their beliefs and assumptions will affect their research.

- Large-scale research projects are not necessarily better than small-scale projects.

- The researcher needs to address ethical issues including the confidentiality of data collected and gaining the relevant consents.

■ ■ ■ Final conclusions

Research is fundamental to developing an understanding of our work as teachers and what happens in the classroom. Practitioner research is most likely to thrive in contexts that support a culture of enquiry, encourage collaborative working, respect the voices and knowledge of teachers and recognize the optimal condition as being one where the teacher researcher has autonomy within their research. Practitioners need to follow where their curiosity leads and seek answers to questions in whatever way they can. Texts, such as this one, outline some of the possible methodologies that can be employed but resourceful teachers will find others. In effect each researcher needs to devise their own unique tools for their research and not be put off by the rhetoric that can surround academic research. Research is part of learning and is automatic in what teachers and pupils do. It is precisely this combination of learning and professional development that is at the heart of practitioner research.

Dadds and Hart (2001) show how innovative research methodologies, such as the use of visualization, conversation and fictional accounts as methods of enquiry and reporting, can elicit fascinating insights into aspects of education. Stepping outside established methodologies requires both practitioners and their mentors or supervisors to be brave and bold in the face of potential criticism from traditionalists. This is an excellent time to take this step, when the UK government is funding teacher practitioner research projects, when more and more is being learned internationally about the value of such research to teachers' professional identity and development, and when there is an increasing realization that creativity at all levels is key to progress.

Zeichner (2003: 320) counsels that this type of professional development 'represents long-term investment in building the capacity of teachers to exercise their judgement and leadership abilities to improve learning for themselves and their students. It is not a form of teacher education that produces quick fixes for complex and enduring problems in schooling'.

■ ■ ■ Task: Designing and critically appraising a small-scale research project

This is a collation of tasks carried out at the end of previous chapters.

1. Identify a focus for a proposed research project. Justify the focus using literature as appropriate.
2. Clearly state title and research questions.
3. Relate the proposed research to paradigms.
4. Identify a list of appropriate literature.
5. List the methods to be used, the intended respondents, and the form of the data to be obtained. This section could be taken further by designing and piloting the actual research tools.
6. Identify any limitations of the proposal.

Having completed the above you should be in a position to conduct your research project.

■ ■ ■ References

Aldrich, F. and Sheppard, L. (2000) '"Graphicacy": the fourth "R"?', *Primary Science Review*, 64: 8–11.

Aldridge, A. and Levine, K. (2001) *Surveying the Social World*. Buckingham: Open University Press.

Altrichter, H., Posch, P. and Somkeh, B. (1993) *Teachers Investigate their Work: An Introduction to the Methods of Action Research*. London: Routledge.

Anderson, G. with Arsenault, N. (1998) *Fundamentals of Educational Research*. London: Falmer Press.

Arksey, H. and Knight, P. (1999) *Interviewing for Social Scientists*. London: Sage.

Avis, J. (2001) 'Educational research, the teacher researcher and social justice', *Education and Social Justice*, 3(3): 34–42.

Bartlett, S. (2002) 'An evaluation of the work of a group of best practice researchers', *Journal of In-service Education*, 28(3): 527–40.

Bartlett, S. and Burton, D. (eds) (2003) *Education Studies: Essential Issues*. London: Sage.

Bartlett, S., Burton, D. and Peim, N. (2001) *Introduction to Education Studies*. London: Paul Chapman Publishing.

Bassey, M. (1990) 'On the nature of research in education (part 2)', *Research Intelligence* 37, Summer: 39–44.

Bassey, M. (1998) 'Action research for improving educational practice', in R. Halsall, (ed.), *Teacher Research and School Improvement: Opening Doors from the Inside*. Buckingham: Open University Press.

Becker, H. (1962) 'The nature of a profession', *Yearbook – National Society for the Study of Education*, 61, pt 2: 27–46.

Becker, H. (1963) *Outsiders: Studies in the Sociology of Deviance*. New York: Free Press.

Bell, J. (1999) *Doing Your Research Project: A Guide for First-Time Researchers in Education and Social Science.* Buckingham: Open University Press.

Blaxter, L., Hughes, C. and Tight, M. (2001) *How to Research.* Buckingham: Open University Press.

Bottery, M. (1996) 'The challenge to professionals from the new public management: implications for the teaching profession', *Oxford Review of Education,* 22(2): 179–97.

Bottery, M. and Wright, N. (1999) 'The directed profession: teachers and the state in the third millennium', a paper submitted at the Annual SCETT Conference, Dunchurch, November.

Bowles, S. and Gintis, H. (1976) *Schooling in Capitalist America: Educational Reform and the Contradictions of Economic Life.* London: Routledge and Kegan Paul.

British Educational Research Association (BERA) (2003a) 'Ethical guidelines for educational research: consultation of members', *Research Intelligence,* no. 82, Southwell, Notts: BERA.

British Educational Research Association (BERA) (2003b) *Issues and Principles in Educational Research for Teachers,* Southwell, Notts: BERA.

Bryant, I. (1996) 'Action research and reflective practice', in D. Scott and R. Usher (eds), *Understanding Educational Research.* London: Routledge.

Burgoyne, J. (1994) 'Stakeholder analysis', in C. Cassell and G. Symon (eds), *Qualitative Methods in Organisational Research: A Practical Guide.* London: Sage.

Burton, D. (2001) 'Ways pupils learn', in S. Capel, M. Leask and T. Turner (eds), *Learning to Teach in the Secondary School,* 2nd edn. London: Routledge.

Burton, D. and Bartlett, S. (2002) 'The professional nature of teaching: issues for design and technology teachers', in S. Sayers, J. Morley and B. Barnes (eds), *Issues in Design and Technology Teaching.* London: RoutledgeFalmer.

Burton, D. and Bartlett, S. (2002) 'The implications of performance management for teacher professional'. A paper presented at the British Educational Research Association Conference, Exeter, 11–14 September.

Campbell, A. (2002) 'Research and the professional self', in O. McNamara (ed.) *Becoming an Evidence-Based Practitioner: A Framework for Teacher Researchers.* London: RoutledgeFalmer.

Carr, W. and Kemmis, S. (1986) *Becoming Critical: Education, Knowledge and Action Research.* London: Falmer Press.

Carter, K. (1998) 'School effectiveness and school improvement', in R. Halsall (ed.), *Teacher Research and School Improvement: Opening Doors from the Inside.* Buckingham: Open University Press.

Carter, K. and Halsall, R. (1998) 'Teacher research for school improvement', in R. Halsall (ed.), *Teacher Research and School Improvement: Opening Doors from the Inside.* Buckingham: Open University Press.

Chapman, V.L. (1999) 'A woman's life remembered: autoethnographic reflections of an adult/educator', paper presented at SCUTREA 29th Annual Conference, 5–7 July, University of Warwick.

Clandinin, J.D. and Connelly, M.F. (1994) 'Personal experience methods', in N.K. Denzin and Y.S. Lincoln (eds), *The Handbook of Qualitative Research.* Newbury Park, CA: Sage

Clough, P. (2002) *Narratives and Fictions in Educational Research.* Buckingham: Open University Press.

Clough, P. and Nutbrown, C. (2002) *A Student's Guide to Methodology.* London: Sage.

Cohen, L., Manion, L. and Morrison, K. (2000) *Research Methods in Education.* 5th edn. London: Routledge Falmer.

Corbetta, P. (2003) *Social Research: Theory, Methods and Techniques.* London: Sage.

Creemers, B. (1994) 'The history, value and purpose of school effectiveness studies', in D. Reynolds, B. Creemers, P. Nesselrodt, E. Schaffer, S. Stringfeld and C. Teddlie (eds), *Advances in School Effectiveness Research and Practice.* Oxford: Pergamon.

Cuff, E. and Payne, G., with Francis, D., Hustler, D. and Sharrock, W. (1984) *Perspectives in Sociology.* 2nd edn. London: Allen and Unwin.

Dadds, M. and Hart, S. (2001) *Doing Practitioner Research Differently.* London: RoutledgeFalmer

Deming, W. (1986) *Out of the Crisis: Quality, Productivity and Competitive Position.* Cambridge: Cambridge University Press.

Department for Education and Employment (DfEE) (1997) *Excellence in Schools.* London: The Stationery Office.

Department for Education and Employment (DfEE) (1998) *Teachers Meeting the Challenge of Change.* London: The Stationery Office.

Department for Education and Employment (DfEE) (1999) *A Fast Track for Teachers.* London: DfEE Publications Centre.

Department for Education and Employment (DfEE) (2000a) *Professional Development: Support for Teaching and Learning.* London: DfEE Publications Centre.

Department for Education and Employment (DfEE) (2000b) *Best Practice Research Scholarships.* Guidance Notes for Teacher Applicants. London: DfEE Publications Centre.

Department for Education and Employment (DfEE) (2000c) *Performance Management in Schools. Performance Management Framework.* London: DfEE Publications Centre.

Department for Education and Skills (DfES) (2001) *Schools Achieving Success.* London: DfES Publications.

Docking. J. (ed.) (2000) *New Labour's Policies for Schools: Raising the Standard.* London: David Fulton.

Douglas, J.W.B. (1964) *The Home and the School.* St Albans: Panther.

Drever, E. (1995) *Using Semi-Structured Interviews in Small-Scale Research: A Teacher's Guide.* Edinburgh: Scottish Council for Research in Education.

Drever, E. and Cope, P. (1999) 'Students' use of theory in an initial teacher education programme', *Journal of Education for Teaching,* 25(2): 97–109.

Durkheim, E. (1964) *The Rules of Sociological Method.* New York: Free Press.

Durkheim, E. (1970) *Suicide: A Study in Sociology.* London: Routledge and Kegan Paul.

Ebbutt, D., Robson, R. and Worral, N. (2000) 'Educational research partnerships', *Teacher Development,* 4(3): 319–37.

Edwards, R. and Usher, R. (2000) *Globalisation and Pedagogy: space, place and identity.* London: Routledge.

Elliott, J. (1991) *Action Research for Educational Change.* Milton Keynes: Open University Press.

Elliott, J. (1996) 'School effectiveness research and its critics: alternative visions of schooling', *Cambridge Journal of Education,* 26(2): 199–223.

Elliott, J. (1998) *The Curriculum Experiment: Meeting the Challenge of Social Change.* Buckingham: Open University Press.

Elliott, J. (2001) 'Making evidence-based practice educational', in *British Educational Research Journal,* 27(5): 555–74.

Elliott, J. (2003) Interview with John Elliott, 6 December 2002, *Educational Action Research,* 11(2): 169–80.

EPPI-Centre (2003) 'About the EPPI-Centre'. http://eppi.ioe.ac.uk/EPPIWeb/home.aspx.

Evans, M., Lomax, P. and Morgan, H. (2000) 'Closing the circle: action research partnerships towards better learning and teaching in schools'. *Cambridge Journal of Education,* 30(3): 405–20.

Fawcett, M. (1996) *Learning Through Child Observation.* London: Jessica Kingsley.

Flick, U. (2002) *An Introduction to Qualitative Research*. London: Sage.

Freeman, J. (1998) *Educating the Very Able: Current International Research. OFSTED Reviews of Research*. London: The Stationery Office.

Glaser, B. and Strauss, A. (1967) *The Discovery of Grounded Theory*. Chicago, IL: Aldane.

Goffman, E. (1971) *The Presentation of Self in Everyday Life*. London: Penguin.

Gomm, R., Hammersley, M. and Forster, P. (eds) (2000) *Case Study Method: Key Issues, Key Texts*. London: Sage.

Grace, G. (1995) *School Leadership: Beyond Educational Management*. London: Falmer Press.

Greenbank, P. (2003) 'The role of values in educational research: the case for reflexivity', *British Educational Research Journal* 29(6): 791–801.

Habermas, J. (1974) *Theory and Practice*, transl. John Viertel. London: Heinemann.

Halsall, R. (2001) 'School improvement: an overview of key findings', in R. Halsall (ed.) *Teacher Research and School Improvement: Opening Doors from the Inside*. Buckingham: Open University Press.

Hammersley, M. (2002) *Educational Research, Policymaking and Practice*. London: Paul Chapman Publishing.

Hammersley, M. and Atkinson, I. (1995) *Ethnography: Principles in Practice*. 2nd edn. London: Routledge.

Hammersley, M. and Gomm, R. (2000) Introduction in R. Gomm, M. Hammersley and P. Foster (eds), *Case Study Method*. London: Sage.

Hannan, A., Enright, H. and Ballard, P. (2000) 'Using research: the results of a pilot study comparing teachers, general practitioners and surgeons'. Available at: http://www.leeds.ac.uk/educol/documents/000000851.

Hargreaves, D. (1996) *Teaching as a Research Based Profession: Possibilities and Prospects*, The Teacher Training Agency Annual Lecture, Birmingham.

Harris, D.L. and Anthony, H.M. (2001) 'Collegiality and its role in teacher development: perspectives from veteran and novice teachers', *Teacher Development*, 5(3): 371–89.

Hart, C. (2001) *Doing a Literature Search*. London: Sage.

Hayes, D. (2000) *The Handbook for Newly Qualified Teachers*. London: David Fulton.

Heaney, S. (2001) 'Experience of induction in one local education authority', *Mentoring and Tutoring*, 9(3): 241–54.

Hillage, J., Pearson, R., Anderson, A. and Tamkin, P. (1998) *Excellence in Research on Schools* (Hillage Report). London: Department of Education and Employment.

Hitchcock, G. and Hughes, D. (1995) *Research and the Teacher*. 2nd edn. London: Routledge.

Hopkins, D. (2001) *School Improvement for Real*. London: RoutledgeFalmer.

Hopkins, D. (2002) *A Teacher's Guide to Classroom Research*. 3rd edn. Buckingham: Open University Press.

Hopkins, D. and Harris, A. (2000) *Creating the Conditions for Teaching and Learning*. London: David Fulton.

Hoyle, E. (1980) 'Professionalisation and deprofessionalisation in education', in E. Hoyle and J. Megarry (eds), *World Yearbook of Education 1980: Professional Development of Teachers*. London: Kogan Page.

Hoyle, E. (1995) 'Changing conceptions of a profession', in H. Busher and R. Saran (eds), *Managing Teachers as Professionals in Schools*. London: Kogan Page.

Jensen, A.R. (1973) *Educational Differences*. London: Methuen.

Kemmis, S. and Wilkinson, M. (1998) 'Participatory action research and the study of practice', in B. Atweh, S. Kemmis and P. Weeks, P. (eds), *Action Research in Practice*. London: Routledge.

Kraft, N. (2002) 'Teacher research as a way to engage in critical reflection: a case study', *Reflective Practice*, 3(2): 175–90.

Krueger, R. (1994) *Focus Groups. A Practical Guide*, 2nd edn. Thousand Oaks, CA: Sage.

Lewin, K. (1946) 'Action research and minority problems. *Journal of Social Issues*, 2: 34–6.

Lewis, I. and Munn, P. (1997) *So You Want to Do Research! A Guide for Beginners on how to Formulate Research Questions*. Edinburgh: SCRE.

Local Education Authorities Project (LEAP) (1991) *Appraisal in Schools*. Milton Keynes: BBC.

Mackintosh, M. (1998) 'Learning from photographs', in S. Scoffham (ed.), *Primary Sources: Research Findings in Primary Geography*, Sheffield: Geographical Association.

Mansell, W. (2001) 'Performance pay saps teacher morale', *Times Educational Supplement*, 21 September.

Maykut, P. and Morehouse, R. (1994) *Beginning Qualitative Research*. London: Falmer Press.

McCulloch, G. (2001) 'The reinvention of teacher professionalism', in R. Philips and J. FURLONG (eds), *Education, Reform and the State. Twenty-five Years of Politics, Policy and Practice*. London: RoutledgeFalmer.

McNally, J., Boreham, N., Cope, P. and Stronach, I. (2003) 'Researching early professional learning', paper presented at Annual BERA Conference, 11–13 September, Edinburgh.

McNamara, O. (2002) 'Evidence–based practice through practice-based evidence', in O. McNamara (ed.), *Becoming an Evidence-Based Practitioner: A Framework for Teacher-Researchers*. London: RoutledgeFalmer.

McNamara, O. and Rogers, B. (2002) 'Introduction: inviting research,' in O. McNamara (ed.), *Becoming an Evidence-Based Practitioner: A Framework for Teacher-Researchers*. London: RoutledgeFalmer.

McNiff, J. (1988) *Action Research: Principles and Practice*. London: Macmillan.

McNiff, J., with Whitehead, J. (2002) *Action Research: Principles and Practice*. 2nd edn. London: RoutledgeFalmer.

Miles, M. and Huberman, M. (1994) *Qualitative Data Analysis*. London: Sage.

Miller, N., and West, L. (2003) 'The auto/biographical "we": our search for a voice in academic writing', paper presented at SCUTREA, 33rd annual conference, University of Wales, Bangor, 1–3 July.

Montgomery, D. (1999) *Positive Teacher Appraisal through Classroom Observation*. London: David Fulton.

Munn, P. and Drever, E. (1995) *Using Questionnaires in Small-Scale Research: A Teacher's Guide*. Edinburgh: Scottish Council for Research in Education.

Myers, K. (1992) *Genderwatch! After the Education Reform Act*. Cambridge: Cambridge University Press.

Office for Standards in Education (OFSTED) (2002) *Continuing Professional Development for Teachers in Schools*. London: OFSTED

Oliver, P. (2003) *The Student's Guide to Research Ethics*. Maidenhead: Open University Press.

Oppenheim, A.N. (1966) *Questionnaire Design and Attitude Measurement*. London: Heinemann.

Ozga, J (1995) 'New Age traveller', *Curriculum Studies*, 3(1): 190–5.

Ozga, J. (2000) 'Education: New Labour, new teachers', in J. Clark S. Gewirtz and E. McLaughlin (eds), *New Managerialism, New Welfare?* London: Sage.

Ozga, J. and Lawn, M. (1988) 'Schoolwork: interpreting the labour process of teaching', *British Journal of Sociology of Education*, 9(3): 323–36.

Patrick, F., Forde, C. and McPhee, A. (2003) 'Challenging the "New Professionalism": from managerialism to pedagogy', *Journal of In-service Education*, 29(2): 237–53.

Pole, C. and Lampard, R. (2002) *Practical Social Investigation: Qualitative and Quantitative Methods in Social Research*. London: Prentice Hall.

Powell, G., Chambers, M. and Baxter, G. (2002) *Pathways to Classroom Observation: A Guide for Team Leaders*. Bristol: TLO.

Prior, L. (2003) *Using Documents in Social Research*. London: Sage.

Punch, K. (1998) *Introduction to Social Research: Quantitative and Qualitative Approaches*. London: Sage.

Reynolds, D., Creemers, B., Bird, J., Farrell, S. and Swint, F. (1994) 'School effectiveness – the need for an international perspective', in D, Reynolds, B. Creemers, P. Nesselrodt, E. Schaffer, S. Stringfield and C. Teddlie (eds), *Advances in School Effectiveness Research and Practice*. Oxford: Pergamon.

Rickinson, M., Aspinall, C., Clark, A., Dawson, L., McLoad, S., Poulton, P., Rogers, J. and Sargent, J. (2003) 'Connecting research and practice: education for sustainable development', NFER/GTC/BERA. available at: www.nfer.ac.uk./eur.

Roberts, B. (2002) *Biographical Research*. Buckingham: Open University Press.

Rutter, M., Maughan, B., Mortimore, P. and Oulston, J. (1979) *Fifteen Thousand Hours*. London: Open Books.

Sammons, P., Hillman, J. and Mortimore, P. (1995) *Key Characteristics of Effective Schools: A Review of School Effectiveness Research*. London: Office for Standards in Education.

Scholtes, P. (1998) *The Leaders' Handbook: Making Things Happen, Getting Things Done*. New York: McGraw-Hill.

Schön, D. (1983) *The Reflective Practitioner*. New York: Basic Books.

Scott, D. (1996) 'Ethnography and education', in D. Scott and D. Usher (eds), *Understanding Educational Research*. London: Routledge.

Simpson, M. and Tuson, J. (1995) *Using Observations in Small-Scale Research: A Beginner's Guide*. Edinburgh: Scottish Council for Research in Education.

Squires, G. (1999) *Teaching as a Professional Discipline*. Falmer: London.

Stenhouse, L. (1983) *Authority, Education and Emancipation*. London: Heinemann.

Stott, K. (1994) 'Teaching geography using photographs', unpublished dissertation, Canterbury Christ Church College.

Stronach, I., Corbin, B., McNamara, O., Stark, S. and Warne, T. (2002) 'Towards an uncertain politics of professionalism: teacher and nurse identities in flux',

Journal of Education Policy, 17(1): 109–38.

Sugrue, C. and DAY, C. (eds) (2002) *Developing Teachers and Teaching Practice*. London: RoutledgeFalmer.

Taylor, D. and Proctor, M. (2001) 'The literature review: a few tips on conducting it', University of Toronto. Available at: http://www.utoronto.ca/writing/litrev.html.

Teacher Training Agency (TTA) (1996) *Teaching as a Research-based Profession*. (Prepared by the TTA and the Central Office of Information 3/96. TETR J036294JJ.) London: Teacher Training Agency Information Section.

Teddlie, C. and Reynolds, D. (2000) *International Handbook of School Effectiveness Research*. London: Falmer Press.

Thompson, M. (2000) 'Performance management: new wine in old bottles', *Professional Development Today*, 3(3): 9–19.

Thrupp, M. (2001) 'Recent school effectiveness counter-critiques: problems and possibilities', *British Educational Research Journal*, 27(4): 443–58.

Tooley, J. and Darby, D. (1998) *Educational Research: A Critique*. London: OFSTED.

Usher, R. (1995) 'Telling the story of the self/deconstructing the self of the story', Annual SCUTREA Conference, University of Southampton.

Verma, G. and MALLICK, K. (1999) *Researching Education. Perspectives and Techniques*. London: Falmer Press.

Vygotsky, L.S. (1962) *Thought and Language*. Cambridge, MA: MIT Press.

Vygotsky, L.S. (1978) *Mind in Society: The Development of Higher Psychological Processes*. London: Harvard University Press.

Walford, G. (2001) *Doing Qualitative Educational Research: A Personal Guide to the Research Process*. London: Continuum.

Walsh, M. and Muster, D. (2002) 'Not only, but also ... "hard" and "soft" research stories', in O. McNamara (ed.), *Becoming an Evidence-Based Practitioner: A Framework for Teacher-Researchers*. London: RoutledgeFalmer.

Waterland, L. (2001) 'Not a perfect offering', in M. Dadds and S. Hart *Doing Practitioner Research Differently*, London: RoutledgeFalmer, pp. 121–39.

Webb, P.T. (2002) 'Teacher power, autonomy and accountability', *Teacher Development*, 6(1): 47–61.

Wellington, J. (2000) Educational Research – contemporary issues and practical approaches. London: Continuum.

Wheldall, K. and Merrett, F. (1985) *The Behavioural Approach to Teaching Package*. Birmingham: Positive Products.

Whitty, G. (1999) 'Teacher professionalism in new times', a paper submitted to the Annual SCETT Conference, Dunchurch, November.

Whitty, G. (2002) *Making Sence of Education Policy.* London: Paul Chapman Publishing.

Willmott, R. (1999) 'School effectiveness research: an ideological commitment?', *Journal of Philosophy of Education*, 33(2): 253–67.

Woods, P. (1999) *Successful Writing for Qualitative Researchers.* London: Routledge.

Yates, S. (2004) *Doing Social Science Research.* London: Sage/Open University Press.

Yin, R. (2003) *Case Study Research: Design and Methods.* 3rd edn. Thousand Oaks, CA: Sage.

Zeichner, K.M. (2003) 'Teacher research as professional development for P-12 educators in the USA', *Educational Action Research*, 11(2): 301–26.

■ ■ ■ Index

Added to a page number 'f' denotes a figure.